T3-BIE-014

Saving Appearances

Duxbury Press Series in Politics

General Editor

Bernard C. Hennessy
California State College, Hayward

Saving Appearances

The Reestablishment
of Political Science

Henry S. Kariel

Duxbury Press
North Scituate, Massachusetts
Belmont, California

Duxbury Press
A Division of Wadsworth Publishing Company, Inc.

© 1972 by Wadsworth Publishing Company, Inc., Belmont, California 94002. All rights reserved. No part of this book may be reproduced, stored in a retrieval system, or transcribed, in any form or by any means, electronic, mechanical, photocopying, recording, or otherwise, without the prior written permission of the publisher, Duxbury Press, a division of Wadsworth Publishing Company, Inc., Belmont, California.

L.C. Cat. Card No.: 72–78901
ISBN 0–87872–039–1
Printed in the United States of America
1 2 3 4 5 6 7 8 9 10–76 75 74 73 72

Acknowledgment is made for permission to reprint portions of "Creating Political Reality," *American Political Science Review,* December 1970; "The Uses of Policy Analysis," in James C. Charlesworth ed., *Integration of the Social Sciences through Policy Analysis* (Philadelphia: American Academy of Political and Social Science, 1972); "Disarming Political Science," *Polity,* Autumn 1972; and part of "In Search of North America," by Clifford Geertz, *The New York Review,* 16 (April 22, 1971), pp. 22–24.

LIBRARY
ALMA COLLEGE
ALMA, MICHIGAN

*For those—each of them—who
have reduced one another's loneliness
without insisting on anything to
show for it*

LIBRARY
ALMA COLLEGE
ALMA, MICHIGAN

Contents

"But how do you know when a path has no heart, don Juan?"

"Before you embark on it you ask the question: Does this path have a heart? If the answer is no, you will know it, and then you must choose another path."

"But how will I know for sure whether a path has a heart or not?"

"Anybody would know that. The trouble is nobody asks the question; and when a man finally realizes that he has taken a path without a heart, the path is ready to kill him. At that point very few men can stop to deliberate, and leave the path."

"How should I proceed to ask the question properly, don Juan?"

"Just ask it."

"I mean, is there a proper method, so I would not lie to myself and believe the answer is yes when it really is no?"

"Why would you lie?"

"Perhaps because at the moment the path is pleasant and enjoyable."

"That is nonsense. A path without a heart is never enjoyable. You have to work hard even to take it. On the other hand, a path with heart is easy; it does not make you work at liking it."

—Carlos Castaneda
"The Teachings of Don Juan" (1968)

I

The Finality of Beginnings

The intentions which give shape and life to this volume were first outlined by me in a memorandum to graduate students enrolled in two seminars, one at Columbia University and the other at the University of Hawaii:

> *Our concern will be with ways of extending the boundaries of political science—that is, either with making the dominant paradigm of political science more various, open, and exciting or with transcending it by incorporating its useful components in a new paradigm. Notwithstanding the utopian affirmations of such writers as Norman O. Brown or Roland Barthes, I am assuming that there is no ultimate transcendence, no jump into freedom, no escape from paradigms. We may aim to free ourselves from ideology and write at degree zero, paint white on white, compose resounding silences, or blueprint empty analytical frameworks. We may feel drawn to the door held open by R. D. Laing, the agraphia of Rimbaud, or the desperate negations of Nietzsche—especially since these promise to do justice to a polymorphous existence without hierarchy, grammar, etiquette, or police. Yet there is no escaping form.*

> *But since not all forms are equally compelling, it is desirable to make choices, to act. Current political science, however, is less a form of action than reaction, response, repercussion. Others call the shots. To become aware of*

1

the possibilities of an active political science, I would first have us identify how political science is institutionally as well theoretically constrained today. One strategy for becoming critical is to inquire into the ideological functions of political science literature of various persuasions. Another is to imagine alternatives. In any case, I should like to proceed dialectically, beginning as naively as possible with present experiences within the discipline. Boredom and embarrassment should then impel us to move ahead.

You should first make yourself familiar with . . .

And so it went in a conventional academic idiom designed to induce students to frame the questions which have become the basis of my attempt to redraw boundaries, to capture some new territory—or perhaps merely to reclaim some that is old.

Despite modish talk about interdisciplinary work, the boundaries of political science are not generously drawn. Beyond the edge of certainty, there are whirls of grimy flotsam and refuse—all politics—peculiar, puzzling stuff untouched by clean hands and disciplined minds. Those who aspire to become professionals learn to trim their interests, and few over thirty are left with the emotional resources to break out. Estranged from history and law, ignorant of science and mathematics, unaffected by poetry and philosophy, political science nevertheless manages to maintain its momentum by capitalizing on such ancient terms as "politics" and "justice," making promises about the body of scientific knowledge still to come, and exploiting the ability of many of its practitioners to triumph over its rigors. The paperbacks used to *supplement* the central texts of introductory courses are sufficient to expose the narrowness of the discipline: they are written by novelists, dramatists, and journalists—or else by individuals whose experience is less vicarious, who have more directly encountered prison guards, U.S. marshals, university administrators, corporation boards, or welfare officers. The center of political science is located at a considerable remove from the public predicaments of our era, of *any* era.

There is good reason, I think, for attempting to make po-

2

litical science relevant—relevant not to Women's Lib or Black Power or Clean Air or the Counter Culture, but to the larger contexts of specific social currents, to the public ground that gives significance to our private acts. To establish the meaning of the events of the times, there is no avoiding efforts to redefine political knowledge—political science. Nothing less will do, I believe, than to rehabilitate it as a comprehensive master science, as an architectonic discipline concerned with relating (in both senses) the seemingly unrelated, untold interests of society, with giving a measure of meaning to our mindless preoccupations, with following C. Wright Mills's advice to transform private troubles into public issues.

A reconstituted discipline would, I think, demote practitioners who are unnerved by political phenomena (whether in themselves or in their field of inquiry). And it would welcome sociologists, anthropologists, economists, social psychologists, and others whose attachment to politics finds expression in

> *In order to make our lives unique, to make them meaningful, to transcend the ordinary — in order to talk about experiences that are otherwise mundane and commonplace, within the understanding of all men, we employ language that is oblique, vague, abstract, indirect. And suddenly we have something, possess something, see something that goes beyond experience, that creates the possibility of, indeed defines, a new reality.*
>
> —A. Weil
> "Recessions" (1971)

their performances—in their speech acts, their research designs, their published work, their public appearances. In short, those who *practice* what I am seeking to define as political science would emerge as acknowledged political scientists.

Such readiness to embrace nonprofessionals comes easiest, of course, when one departs from a secure base, implies one never leaves one's friends behind, and gets known for delivering

3

as promised. Thus I have always tried to keep my credit rating intact at least by meeting expected deadlines. Yet my loyalties are deeply split, my connections unclear. I have made repeated efforts (first in the early sixties) to depart from the profession of political science by ordering some of my thoughts—the thoughts of others—in language manifestly disconnected, askew, and obscure. I first sought to distinguish between a private and a public sector of experience—convinced they existed as distinct entities, had only to be located and duly tagged. Was there not the possibility, scarcely realized, of a rich private life to be maintained by a constitutional order? I supposed we might always rely on something like the Madisonian system of checks and balances, which has been ritually celebrated by political pluralists beginning with Tocqueville and which continues to permeate the elementary textbooks of political science. True, America had departed from constitutionalism by letting technology generate a centralized network of associations more powerful and less accountable than the state. True, too, American political science had quietly rationalized and glorified this departure. But in what I called a collage, *The Decline of American Pluralism* (1961), I implied we might yet return to the true Constitution, embrace John Locke, Adam Smith, David Hume, and James Madison, our authentic fathers, no others available.

Later, having taken time to review the work of contemporary political thinkers to search for new words as basis for authority, I could still do little but reaffirm the liberal creed: the goal of politics is surely to enable as many individuals as possible to have a richer private existence. This notion began to fade, however, when I subsequently considered the unfulfilled promise of politics, recognizing how curiously *satisfying* it was to inject private, untamed impulses into the political sphere where they might be at once displayed and mastered—mastered *because* displayed. And more recently, under the influence of Nietzsche and two Americans who managed to be simultaneously tough and vulnerable, Herman Melville and Henry Adams, I have sought to push all the way, arguing in *Open Systems* (1969) that we might progressively annihilate the dead ends of privacy and proceed to democratize the public arena—all of us committed to *praxis*, all

4

of us at last emerging as performers, everyone demonstrating, acting, politicking, no one ending except by choice.

But what sort of science — what kind of disciplined knowledge — might testify to such a state of affairs, or at least not demean it? What ways of conducting oneself would *not* do violence to the state as conceived on the one hand by Aristotle and Nietzsche — who agreed that only the few could ever manage to harmonize their conflicting interests — and on the other by Rousseau, Jefferson, Mill, and Dewey, democrats who wanted to let others into the act, who erected no barriers to protect elites, who saw only practical impediments to the triumph of equality? It seemed to me — I was but following European phenomenology and existentialism — that there was no way to knowledge and power without bringing oneself into social acts, without making oneself appear while at the same time laboring on whatever words, disciplines, instruments, and institutions were likely to promote our collective capacity to act, to assure the continuous public appearance of repressed aspects of ourselves. To attend to the whole of man, *all* one might make visible, meant displaying a concern for others, for all living representatives of still private parts of ourselves. And this turned out to involve a kind of surrender, a purge — the elimination of the great liberal distinction between self and others, between private and public. For me, it has slowly become easy to conclude that while there may well be intellectual disciplines aspiring to *less* than that, they cannot claim to be political science. In sum, I can sanction not a retreat from politics to the political scientist's study but rather a definition of political knowledge which fuses it with political practice.

Thus I do not wish to present some useful methodology or provide still another training manual for the ideal political scientist, a preliminary to great projects to come. Instead, I am searching for a posture, a style, a language that might *stop* prevalent ways of talking and get closer to those invisible domains — unrealized possibilities — that touch and move us as political beings.

Of course I realize that in the social sciences it is still difficult to talk about nonevents and nonrealities, to affirm mere appearances. To remain connected and hold readers, it remains

5

necessary to refer to things of substance, to offer solid truths — hard facts — beyond the filigree of precious phrases. I would certainly be offering less substance if I thought I could get away with less. As it is, I am seeking to engage in minimal work, to avoid definitiveness, to establish as little as I can. What sustains me is evidence of changing expectations in the social sciences: solid, trustworthy frameworks are becoming suspect while vulnerable models are gaining in attractiveness.

A growing community of scholars bears witness to the exhaustion of the conventional language for ordering our political life — and knows that they cannot recover experience in silence. As my footnotes indicate, many political scientists have been on the verge of saying what various philosophers have said, and what I am reaffirming here. In some cases, graduate training and professional life have silenced my colleagues. In others, they have feared being misunderstood or not wanted to replace old with new privileges. Many have learned political science so well that they have come to doubt their own ability to remain dialectical and discursive, playful and political.

I share their doubts and make it easy for them to note that I remain attached to the past, still affirming, positing, concluding, not yet abandoning authorship, syntax, margins, footnotes, and good taste. In short, a compromising posture. A bad connection.

If I felt able to act on my professed ideals more fully, I would not be pretending, as I implicitly have been, that to produce this volume I *first* outlined my intentions and *then* proceeded to carry them out. Nor would I pretend to complete a manuscript which shows nothing of its author's tensions, which carefully conceals how one discovers one's intentions and meanings in the process of writing. Instead, I would let the strains show, reveal that I have not finished, that I have worked for an "incomplete," deliberately quit making notes and collecting quotations, composing myself in the end only because I thought it timely to move on, to escape finishing, to begin.

Yet to make one's props explicit throws doubt on the legitimacy of one's performance. To appear disciplined, one must still come up with some creation myth or some final model, constructs designed to conceal experiences which are yet to be

6

acknowledged as meaningful parts of oneself—experiences such as seeking research support, flirting with superiors and subordinates, erecting scaffolding, tuning instruments, staging rehearsals. But why not persist and regard *all* these preparations as performances—even if not publicized as The Real Thing? Should one not destroy one's instruments by bringing them out into the open, displaying them, treating them as if there were nothing else of value?

Unprepared to say yes, political scientists (like others in power) not only speak of "openings" and "closings" but also help to make them official and real. They categorize and reify. They thereby keep outsiders from seeing all that which precedes and follows their lectures, presentations, books, their various public acts. By restricting the meaning of performance, they limit access, make part of life inaccessible. They keep an inside track secret, live their lives off the record, unrecorded.

It may be possible to extend the record slightly. In my high school—it is now Portland State College—someone dramatically broke out of official reality by coming up with what we were to call Chinese theater. During the rehearsal of *Macbeth*, she had us transform the changing of scenery into an act itself. Resenting her failure to get a real part, she talked the rest of the stage crew (and our speech teacher) into leaving up the curtain between acts. The crew learned to play the role of crew, to perform, to put on an act between real acts, a play called *Changing Scenes*. We rehearsed, showed ourselves acting, parodied ourselves, and were finally so buoyed by our work that the real actors—now clearly the *other* actors—were won as audience— ultimately moved to participate in the applause of the real audience.

It is of course clear to me that not everyone played. There was still our teacher, dead serious throughout, not aware of being underprivileged. There were ushers and janitors, men at the top and the bottom, all off stage, leading lives that were private and invisible. Yet would we not ideally extend the range of visibility and get everyone into our act? At best, would we not establish a vantage point from which to perceive all human behavior as performance and from which no arena for public action could be treated as the preserve of the privileged orders of society?

7

Were such a perspective adopted by political scientists, they would be kept from designating some performances as real and all others as unreal, as *mere* rehearsals and preparations, as *mere* means to greater ends. It would keep them from insinuating that what they offer publicly has been (and therefore must be) bounded precisely as they know it to be bounded. It would keep them from believing that every act is an end product. Instead, they would applaud every display of action—even a writer who declines either to begin or end, who is determined to avoid creat-

> *What good is it unless you've got something to show for it?*
>
> —American colloquialism

ing still another Very Important Product fit to be copyrighted, catalogued, shelfed, assigned, cited, and remaindered. They would construct a world in which each act appeared as complete in itself. The conventional means-ends distinction—the belief that *lowly* means must be employed to achieve some *higher* end—would disappear. They would regard nothing whatever as means—no person or curriculum, no therapeutic treatment, revolutionary act, bureaucratic organization, commuting trip, training bout, field work, or scholarly investigation. Everything would be self-fulfilling, intrinsically satisfying.

Of course someone would remind them that when they view our activities as a form of play they are self-indulgent and parochial. Millions can't afford admission to their theater. Millions are hurting. Politics is not for them, not yet. But might political scientists not see all men as already admitted, as playing *but not knowing it?* The practical question is how to make *apparent* non-players conscious of their condition—of the establishable fact that they are but *appearing* as nonplayers, that "nonplaying" is the name of their game. To make others conscious of their potential, I know of only one strategy: you display yourself at play, reveal that you are doing nothing else, that for you nothing is real but the play. It is the act of clowns and saints, confidence men and picaros.[1] Their fate, however, is familiar. When such actors appear in the purest form—unashamed and stripped of all earnestness—they are done to death by the mass of men and those who govern. Whether their elimination is initiated by elites who wish to keep the pleasures of playing to themselves or by the masses, the effect is the same: the actors are kept from appearing. Accordingly, I am quite prepared to pretend that I am serious, that my work is no play, that I am doing something of consequence. Still, I can also let on that I may not be *wholly* serious, that just possibly I am not serious at all—except insofar as an uncontrollable Necessity makes me collide with ineluctable reality.

In short, life as drama is not *consistently* my perspective. If it were, this volume would be more of a disjointed scrap book, something less definitively organized and harder to index, its order dictated not by a predefined objective but by a life as lived, its various arguments not arranged to end somewhere but to reveal every instant that they (and I along with them) have arrived. Unfortunately, my ideal publisher is not yet born. He would contract to publish only the barest traces of my thought and industry—but not The Real Work itself. Of course no sensible publisher could simply accept this role; he would protest, saying that the only way he can assure readers that I actually intended *not* to make a case for anything in the end, that I wanted to arrive *nowhere*, would be by his publishing some distinct *result* of my intentions. But I would question his good sense and resist him, offer no unified result—merely some fragile odds and ends (both) that he might put between covers, much as a collage is assembled and then framed. Everyone would then be pleased to note that the published work could have been quite different, that it did not have to be, that it begs to be changed by whoever might be touched by it.

But again, I can merely lean in this direction. Interested in making the social scientist himself appear within his field of inquiry, I am still keeping at least half of myself somewhere in the background, inadvertently revealing the cost of inhibition. To live up to my professions, I should surely inject a good deal more of myself into this book, using my factual or fictitious past to show how action transforms at once the actor, the world he acts on, and

9

the records of past action. It is not sufficient to confess one's bias in a preface and to keep inserting the first person singular into opinionated passages. What is needed—what it would still cost me too much to supply—is some transcript of my transactions with my environment—with family and friends, students in and out of courses, travel companions and colleagues, friends in the Caucus for a New Political Science, members (none friends) of the Council of the American Political Science Association, others in literary and governmental groups. After all, I have tested (and been a test to) each of them in various ways. One wild, incandescent moment can be made to stand for others since it is safely past. No one else will wish to recall that it had been possible to express the thought (never more than that) that an academic department— all of us visible in Hawaii—might proceed to pool individual incomes, replace secretaries who would not adjust to such a windfall, discard wives or husbands who would not disarm, and recruit no new chairman who would feel otherwise. We would change offices into lounges, clerks into research associates, teachers into students. We would all become untenured participant-observers whirling beyond schedules, unregistered and out of bounds. But while the thought hangs on, sense prevailed as the 1960s ended even in the Pacific. My heroic involvements—midnight defeats— testify to the limits of our endowments. However minimally, my transactions have changed me and my environs—and might provide a record others are bound to subvert insofar as they can treat it as fiction.

Pretending now to be altogether where I am, mainly in "Political Science," I am providing no such account. When I move outside my profession, my existence is surreptitious, unreal, and pseudonymous, devoid of significance for insiders, appreciated only because disguised. This book acquiesces in such professional expectations, though I am nearing the edge, collecting myself for the next project.

Because I mean to bring deflected and underrepresented interests of mine into the open, I am concerned about recognizing persons who themselves manage to represent not only what George Herbert Mead called "significant others" but also others who are insignificant, unperceived, unloved. I should like to create places for such expanded selves within the discipline. Ideally all political scientists would make their appearance within their works, emerging by virtue of their acts. They would thereby become whole and be saved. They would disarm, demonstrate, and perform, invite strangers into their work, create authors and invent quotations—or at least quote more and expand footnotes until unacknowledged borrowings finally permeate their texts and make them social products.

To sustain such a community of political scientists, I am here attempting to sound out—to essay—a viable basis for political action. On this basis, I realize, diverse nonprofessionals have been successfully practicing political science for some time. Journalists, novelists, film directors, historians, anthropologists, sociologists, philosophers, social psychologists, literary critics—all disregarding the alleged value-neutrality of physical science—have in fact been transforming established reality, giving their private visions a compelling political form, activating dormant aspects of our lives. My interest is not, however, just to recognize their work. It is mainly to legitimate projects which duly accredited political scientists might be on the verge of enacting—especially the projects of political scientists who have begun to wonder what they might do when so many things that they do well turn out to be embarrassments.

I cannot help being pleased to have generated the most ambivalent of feelings about the way I have been converting my concerns into words. If four critics of mine who were initially anonymous to me—Mark Roelofs, Bernard Hennessy, Richard Young, and Eldon Eisenach—have changed few of my first thoughts, they are even now compelling me to have second ones, and to keep on writing. For this, precisely, I am grateful. Because I am making a case against authors as solitary individuals, as figures detached from the social landscape, it is easy for me to give recognition to friends, students, and colleagues—fellow players such as Felix Oppenheim, Ian Lind, Lee Seaton, Joan Kincaid, Eugene Miller, Paul Kress, Deane Neubauer, Donna Zucker, Eleanore Chong, Nancy Clemente, Michael J. Shapiro, and John F. Wilson. One way to promote them is by not further blocking publication of their contributions to this volume: the tone they have given it, the quotations they have supplied, the nouns they have eliminated, the verbal traps they have planted. I can best make room for them by moving at least partially out of the way.

II
The Quest for Meaning

A roomful of people, men mainly, a few standing. A flow of subdued, fragmented remarks, muffled and unobtrusive. Ashtrays, pencils, microphones. The film that takes it all in is bound to puzzle. Even when the subject is as relatively familiar as a political proceeding—a legislative hearing, for example—the film is not likely to disclose that those involved are there for some reason, playing meaningful parts conforming to some known pattern. True, legislators or judges or bureaucrats might have arranged themselves in a pleasing manner for the camera, appearing to be judicious and purposeful, wholly in focus, *reasonable*. They might have posed carefully to commemorate the signing of a bill or the swearing in of a new official. Moreover, a flag in the background or a hand on a Bible might reveal the point of the proceedings. But if they have not been moved to appear in some meaningful way, they will seem to be lacking in composure, and the situation captured by the film will appear notably odd. It will have no meaning, too many meanings, or not quite the kind of meaning we would expect. Should we happen to know that the incongruity we witness is of no great consequence, the scene will strike us as comic. On the other hand, if we suspect that it will lead to disastrous effects, we are likely to be dismayed. But however we may be moved by such a scene, what makes it striking is its incongruous nature. We had expected order, but are now witnessing something else. Our expectations being disappointed, we are perplexed.

The more momentous of contemporary public issues have made this feeling of bewilderment familiar enough. Certainly in

13

contemporary America there has been a surfeit of felt incongrui-
ties: much of public life appears to be meaningless. The snap-
shots—whether they cause us to smile or frown or weep—are
plentiful. Some of the scenes are so grotesque as to be virtually
incomprehensible. A country as powerful as the United States
finds itself frustrated by insurgents abroad. A time-honored two-
party system recurrently fails to do justice to the range of alternatives. Public officials operate outside the law as if committed to
anarchy. Policies formulated by regulatory commissions are in-
distinguishable from policies desired by regulated industries.
Programs for the education of the young cripple their creative
powers. The comforts provided by industrial plenty enrage the
presumed beneficiaries. Expressions of altruistic impulses lead
to confrontation, confinement, and a search for cash to get bailed
out. The very legislators who profess concern for the purification
of American life cannot persuade themselves to control corporate
industry so as to make highways less bloody, advertising more
honest, or packaging less deceptive. Where rationality, lawfulness, efficiency, and economy are expected, irrationality, violence,
waste, and brutality are manifest. The entire century, as Michael
Harrington has said, seems to be accidental. In view of well-
identified needs—in the light of publicly professed ideals—
political reality remains senseless: the great formula of political
liberalism fails to make it tolerable. And because we realize that
our public behavior does have significant consequences, few of us
are moved to laughter. Feeling there are public problems, we
demand solutions, or at least explanations. We wonder if new
authorities, leaders, institutions, policies, myths, and theories
might enrich our existence by giving a larger measure of meaning
to our lives. A new consciousness is wanted—or just some old
verities. Mere words would help, provided they are telling ones.

The Norms of Political Science

Political science—a social enterprise designed to give
disciplined expression to the realities and possibilities of political life—may be seen as an organized response to this search.
Today, this is far from obvious because an appreciable number—
probably a growing number—of political scientists are *profes-*

sionally interested less in meeting the crisis of meaning and authority or in making public policy conform to standards of justice than in accumulating knowledge for its own sake. *Professionally*, they are indifferent about the purposes which knowledge might serve, about the meaning it might acquire when policy-makers ultimately employ it to manage and structure political reality. They regard politics as important, but extracurricular.

Nevertheless, not all who would identify themselves as political scientists are preoccupied with developing a pure science. Some display a professional concern which I have had no trouble understanding as their own reaction to perceived strains of public life. The political scientist who is oriented by such a concern is not likely to permit some establishment—political or professional—to identify the problems which beg for solutions. He perceives his environment as more problematic (or differently problematic) than do those in positions of power. As he designs his research and provides descriptive accounts which seek to come to terms with a specific political situation, his very work expresses the unsettled, ambiguous, problematic character of perceived reality. Elucidating political experience, he reveals that present arrangements and present policies—tax laws, national security policy, the budgetary process, for examples—are not only solutions but also problems. Questioning established reality, he calls attention to interests which are eclipsed by prevailing policies or suppressed by governing elites. Troubled by the presumed order of his day—regarding it as a form of disorder—he seeks to recognize distant or invisible interests, to speculate about alternative futures, to conduct experiments demonstrating the functions of new realities, to communicate intuitions of new governmental possibilities, or to bring implicit aspirations into the open. His various activities are intended to heighten consciousness, to subject a maximum range of political life to rational, conscious control.

But what, precisely, constitutes "control"? Can reality be regarded as controlled insofar as we have the power to create or destroy it at will? Is it brought under control the moment it is named, classified, and thus understood? Is it brought under control when we can identify the conditions under which it is perceived and established? Moreover, what are the proper criteria

15

for judging the accuracy and reliability of propositions about reality? And what constitutes *political* reality? What part of reality is to be regarded as nonpolitical, as private or politically irrelevant?

It is apparent, I trust, that the answers to these questions necessarily determine the kind of problems to which political scientists will address themselves. The answers frame the kind of work they will pursue and esteem, the language they use, the research support they request, the books they write, the courses they teach, and the students they attract, train, and recommend for research and teaching positions. In short, the answers to these questions constitute a framework—a paradigm—which directs their professional activities.

This acceptance of paradigmatic directives does not mean, however, that political scientists feel it necessary to reflect on their paradigm every time they embark on some project. They are hardly moved to keep reexamining their premises as they devise

> *The glory of the sciences is their unswerving application of their methods without reflecting on knowledge-constitutive interests. From knowing not what they do methodologically, they are that much surer of their discipline, that is of methodical progress within an unproblematic framework.*
>
> —Jürgen Habermas
> "Technik und Wissenschaft als "'Ideologie'"
> (1968)

new theories, instruments, methodologies, and techniques, or as they plan courses, programs, and research centers. Tacitly agreeing on what it means to do political science properly, they tend to turn directly to their work. An underlying consensus saves time and energy for carrying on professional operations.

To be sure, there will always be deviations from the professional consensus. Some political scientists, secure or bored or inspired, will deliberately wish to strike out in new directions and radically change the given frame of reference. Others may stray simply because they have lost their way. Still others may depart from accepted norms because they anticipate rewards offered by some special interest group. And there may be some who knowingly, mischievously build paradoxes and inconsistencies into their formulations.

Because such deviant behavior is tolerated, I believe it would be misleading to think of political science as a monolithic establishment pervasively governed by a common set of norms. Yet however eclectic the profession, it does remain possible to discern its normative center, a dominant persuasion. Elementary textbooks as well as graduate degree programs readily disclose that some kinds of scholarly activities are more normal and typical than others. Thus one can distinguish the center from the periphery by its style: centrally established activities tend to be carried on in a spirit of dispassionate calmness, not to say complacency. There is much drive and energy, yet little strain. The work may exhaust, but will not agonize. Its authors, taking the ultimate importance of their work for granted, need not trouble themselves with formulating personal justifications for it. Confident that their research will ultimately find its proper place in the body of scientific knowledge, they are free to ignore problems and challenges which emerge at the margin of their discipline. Offering their conclusions without feeling pressed to defend the premises of their work, they accept the consensus of a community of scholars. Their professional behavior, in a word, is conventional.

Categories as Organizers of Reality

This pattern is by no means peculiar to the institution of political science. That the limits of meaningful reality, the choice of relevant problems, and the appropriate techniques for dealing with them are conditioned by social convention in *all* intellectual disciplines was first comprehensively expressed by the work of Immanuel Kant in the eighteenth century. Kant maintained that men cannot under any humanly conceivable circumstances gain objective knowledge of reality "as such," in itself. All we can reasonably claim is that reality conforms to the categories in *our* minds, that is, to the mental constructs which empower men to

17

accommodate reality, to appropriate it and make it theirs.[1] Accordingly, we may never claim to have knowledge of phenomena as such—only "categorical knowledge." For example, without some publicly constructed notion of beginning and end, cause and effect, or of climax and sequence, we could never frame and organize the flow of experience. Without being framed and organized, events would have no significance for us. Our experience, our sheer enduring over time, would be utterly meaningless. It is man's language which bestows meaning on what he then calls reality, which makes "reality" serve his purposes by giving names to the various ways he experiences it. The purpose he has in mind will determine whether he conceptualizes a specific phenomenon as a "school" or as a "prison," associating it with one or the other. That is, his purposes, intentions, interests, and values will induce him to frame and label his experience, for these induce him either to become conceptually inventive or to apply familiar concepts (such as "dramatic performance" or "irresponsible behavior") to new situations (such as an urban riot).

The extent to which purposes themselves are man-made and therefore changeable is not always obvious. We tend to feel that our words refer to a hard and fast reality, to self-defining facts which somehow carry their own meaning. Thus when we are in-

> *The reality we seek is so called only as the terminus of the cognitive process. Appearance is what is to be known; reality, what it is known as.*
>
> —Abraham Kaplan
> "The Conduct of Inquiry" (1964)

tent on keeping others from using our property for public purposes, we will insist that whatever others may believe it to be, it is *really* "private." Someone else with different interests, of course, will insist that no, it is *really* "public"—established because it follows one of the forms of the verb "to be." Yet despite

18

someone's claim about the real nature of property or anything else, we are not justified in assuming that he is objective in referring to the world of reality. What property "really" is, men simply do not know in any disinterested, value-neutral, objective way—though the power they have (including the power to reason) may *establish* it as "public" or "private."

Our interests, it should be clear, lead us to compare and categorize—to classify and have knowledge of property as really private, children as irresponsible, Americans as peace-loving, juries as just, products as goods, or competitiveness as healthy. Concealed similes and metaphors, all originally related to some human purpose, direct our attention. They make us perceptive and discriminating. Languages, logical systems, analytical frameworks, and scientific concepts—symbols generally—organize the world about us.[2] They give us the world we know, the world we then find convenient to accept as given. We cannot gain knowledge, in other words, unless we interact with so-called reality, impose our categories on it so as to make it serve some purpose. Acting in relation to some purpose, we compel reality to make its appearance.

To know reality, Kant wrote in *The Critique of Pure Reason,* men must not approach it "in the manner of a student who listens to all his master chooses to tell him," but instead in the manner of "a judge who compels witnesses to reply to those questions which he himself thinks fit to ask." Historical accounts and scientific findings, it should be evident, can be no more than the result of the questions we pose. It follows that as long as we remain imaginative and ingenious and alive enough to make up new questions, all testimony about social reality must be subject to change. We should therefore not feel constrained by the answers— the very worlds—which have been given us. Since they are merely provisional, since reality is a precarious construction, we are free to keep raising questions that continue to put reality to the test and that continue to restructure it.

Yet our freedom to construct reality, literally to make history, is disconcertingly limited. Absorbed by Kant—forgetting how revolutions are betrayed, how an implacable nature cheats us of our victories, how in the end we die—we readily get carried away: we begin to think expansively of man as the autonomous creator of his environment, indeed, as self-made, wholly constructed in his image, conforming to his ideal. But as Doctor Johnson implied, the pain in one's stubbed toe (not to mention major catastrophes) would seem enough to qualify Kantian idealism and bring us down to a less intoxicating, more "realistic" view of the world. Nor are our encounters with an intractable physical environment the only limits on human creativity and self-assertiveness. Social pressures of which we are only barely aware keep us from raising new questions and hence from reconstructing reality. Born into a society, men absorb its language, its symbol systems, its entire view of the world.[3] This may be seen dramatically in the case of the Hopi Indians, whose language, as Benjamin Lee Whorf pointed out, does not permit them to share conventional Western notions of time and space. For them, a fundamentally different set of concepts discloses a fundamentally different universe. Demonstrating how language shapes ideas and how ideas give shape to nature, Whorf concluded:

> *Formulation of ideas is not an independent process, strictly rational in the old sense, but is part of a particular grammar, and differs, from slightly to greatly, between different grammars. We dissect nature along lines laid down by our native languages. The categories and types that we isolate from the world of phenomena we do not find there because they stare every observer in the face; on the contrary, the world is present in a kaleidoscopic flux of impressions which has to be organized by our minds — and this means largely by the linguistic systems in our minds. We cut nature up, organize it into concepts, and ascribe significances as we do, largely because we are parties to an agreement that holds throughout our speech community and is codified in the patterns of our language. The agreement is, of course, an implicit and unstated one, BUT ITS TERMS ARE ABSOLUTELY OBLIGATORY: we cannot talk at all except by subscribing to the organization and classification of data which the agreement decrees.[4]*

Different grammars, Whorf noted, generate different observations; and different observations, different realities. The concept of "space" evokes one reality for an association of psychologists and another for an association of physicists. "Politics" has different meanings for Democrats than Republicans. More basically, concepts that Kant had still treated as intrinsic to all thinking, regardless of time or place or culture, thus emerge as variable conventions, as mere usages which men might feel free to change. The very center of our thinking becomes unstable—subject only to the order we feel empowered to impose.

Though we are free to coin words or to arrange old ones in new ways, our language is almost wholly "given." Established linguistic convention‑ defeat us as we seek to create new meanings and challenge usage: the poet's assault on prevailing linguistic structures is easily deflected. The world *of* constructs, the world maintained *by* constructs, is such a massive presence that it is readily embraced as something objective and impregnable—along with the purposes which gave rise to it in the first place. Our terms tend to be given (as Hegel said) in the form of master ideas which permeate historical epochs. They may be given by an economic class to protect its privileges (as Marx said), by a priesthood to conceal its weakness from a class of warriors (Nietzsche), or by groups struggling to get or keep power (Mannheim). We easily forget that languages are instruments used in the pursuit of conflicting objectives. "However fully developed our nomenclature is," Goethe noted in his *Diary*, "we must remember that it is only nomenclature; that a word is merely a sign of syllables attached to a certain phenomenon. Thus it can never express nature completely and ought to be regarded as mere equipment for our comfort." We may insist that our words truly identify reality; we may assert that a phenomenon really *is* something or other; we may claim to have knowledge. But our knowledge is inescapably fiction, illusion, myth, ideology, and rationalization.[5]

From this it does not follow, however, that one fiction—or one scientific theory—is as good (or bad) as another. If the root, in Marx's metaphor, is man, to relate theories to man is to make it possible to be discriminating, for it can be shown that some theories are more apt to serve human needs than others. Admittedly, man is not a fixed, predetermined being: his needs and purposes

21

are in a process of change. He is capable of development, of making increasingly effective use of his capacities. He sets ever new tasks for himself, creates new life styles, and imagines new possibilities for meaningful action. But aware of the centrality of his protean nature and wishing to sustain it, hoping to keep him in action—to activate him as fully as possible—we may yet note that some theories are demonstrably more useful than others, and that *those will be most useful which maximize man's range of manageable experience.* To enhance the significance of their lives, men must therefore choose constructs in the manner of Kant's judge, bringing previously insignificant, unused parts of reality into their consciousness. To accommodate their needs, they must favor views of reality which extend the sphere of meaningful action.

The Social Basis of Scientific Revolutions

How scientific views of reality are inextricably linked with the actions and purposes of scientists themselves has become familiar thanks to Thomas S. Kuhn's *Structure of Scientific Revolutions* (1962). His study has served to challenge the generally held belief that physical scientists, as members of a homogeneous community engaged in a common enterprise, have been contributing to a steadily growing body of confirmed, impersonal knowledge. According to Kuhn, scientific enterprises are not launched by any single set of assumptions about the nature and accessibility of reality. Seen in the light of history, scientists have acted in reference to ever-changing presuppositions—paradigms—to identify relevant problems. Since paradigms change, what is relevant during one era becomes irrelevant during another.

At any one time, however, there is likely to be a dominant set of scientific conventions which governs the community of science: a widely shared commitment to working in certain ways within specified boundaries. Like great religious myths or political ideologies, a scientific paradigm compels the loyalty of individual practitioners. Giving meaning to their various activities, it mobilizes, organizes, and directs them. Oriented by a paradigm, scientists will use and perfect their instruments to look in designated places. And there they perceive what different assumptions, different concepts, different criteria for proof—that is, different

22

paradigms—fail to reveal. They not only come to conceptualize a new reality (which, if this were all, might simply be added to confirmed knowledge of the old); they also come to know the previously perceived reality in a new way. The old order of facts is reevaluated—and it acquires a new meaning.

Yet the new meaning, too, will ultimately be challenged. Bored by mere puzzle-solving or by easy successes, perhaps intrigued by accidentally perceived phenomena, some scientists will inevitably be led to question the scientific consensus. Developing new procedures and instruments on their own, they may display an order of facts with which the old paradigm simply cannot cope. As the new vision presents anomalies, the beliefs of other scientists, especially those already working on the fringes of the scientific community, may gradually be shaken. They may begin to see cracks in the familiar system, debate fundamentals, become increasingly radical, and possibly join in a scientific revolution. Such revolutions, in Kuhn's words, are "those non-cumulative developmental episodes in which an older paradigm is replaced in whole or in part by an imcompatible new one."[6]

Understandably, new paradigms are not likely to be embraced as a matter of course by the community of scientists. Before its members will proceed to participate (as Kuhn has put it) in forcing nature into the new conceptual boxes, the new boxes must strike them as extraordinarily enticing. Only the stunningly promising reconstructions of reality of a Copernicus, Newton, Lavoisier, Darwin, or Einstein are apt to shake scientific conventions, making the old way of viewing man and nature seem obsolete. This does not always mean that as a result of a revolutionary breakthrough the problems identified by the old paradigm are solved but rather that problems are now framed in a sufficiently novel and exciting way to activate the community of scientists.

Because there is no assurance of the success of the new paradigm, those scientists who transfer their allegiance to it necessarily take risks. They must decide to practice science in a new way at a time when the new paradigm is still inexact and unaccredited. While the old paradigm successfully dealt with its problems, the new one has hardly begun to cope with the reality it presumes to frame. The decision in its favor is therefore largely an act of faith.

Once the scientific community has become converted, the paradigmatic revolution will run its course: legions of scientists will then enlist in the ranks of what Kuhn has called "normal science." They become involved in puzzle-solving, that is, in dealing with problems known to be soluble in principle. Such normal science consists of mopping-up operations which gradually fulfill the initial promise of the paradigm. Slowly, knowledge of the reality established by the paradigm will be extended, what the paradigm predicts will be stated with greater precision, and the paradigm itself will be further articulated.

Although the activities of scientists may be seen, as I fully realize, from perspectives other than Kuhn's, his interpretation does help clarify the social context and the human concerns of

> *It doesn't matter, at the party afterwards, whether you saw folly or bestiality. Whichever you saw, it only matters how you got it down.*
>
> —Joseph Brakman
> "Films" (1971)

science. His use of such political terms as participation, community, convention, revolution, and loyalty elucidates a view of science not as an impersonal, disinterested form of behavior but as a series of social movements whose participants are quite personally interested in finding solutions to problems—problems defined by them, not nature. If they move toward some goal, it is not a goal provided by reality "out there." If they offer solutions and provide knowledge, this activity is inseparable from their purposes. In other words, the connections, relationships, structures, and patterns which scientific theories attribute to nature are first in the minds of the men whose questions compel nature to respond. The nature which is meaningful for science is therefore always a human construction; it is shaped by men whose imagination empowers them to act, and whose action consists of putting nature to the test.

Yet the campaigns and victories of physical science could hardly be seen in this light until the recent past—that is, until questions began to arise about their effects for good or ill on the human community generally. In the sixteenth century, Francis Bacon had insisted that knowledge is power, and he could plausibly assume that man's power over nature would lead to obviously desirable results. Who would doubt that knowledge was good and more knowledge better? The unleashing of nuclear energy, however, dramatically jeopardized this unspoken agreement. It became apparent, first, that knowledge invariably exists within a specific social context and, second, that when put to use by men in their *present* frame of mind within societies as *now* organized, knowledge would not ineluctably promote everyone's welfare. Some efforts to gain knowledge—certainly those subsidized by dominant groups—could be seen to promote strong and established rather than weak and emergent interests in society. True, mathematics and pure logic might possibly be immune to Marx's charge that science is "class science." But what of the other realms of knowledge? Are not all of them context-bound, relative to specific social groups? Is the search for knowledge ever a disinterested one? Do scientists ever solve problems posed by nature "out there" rather than problems which interest *them*, problems to which they are directed by their interests?

Defining Experience as "Political"

That scientific knowledge must, when applied, affect society in unequal ways—never benefiting all interests equally—is nowhere more evident than in the social sciences. The political scientist can hardly conceal that he has embraced a paradigm for ordering social life which favors some interests in society over those of others. Of course he may profess to be concerned with nothing less lofty than bringing experience under rational control. But what specific range of experience? Doesn't he—or at least someone—have to decide? The relevant range will surely not define itself. Men make choices, and their choices have consequences.

Whatever may be the case today, political thinkers have traditionally chosen to focus on that common order which, as

25

Sheldon Wolin has put it, men deliberately create "to deal with those concerns in which all of the members of society have some interest."[7] Following Aristotle, political thinkers have sought to come to terms with the policies and institutions designed to integrate the full range of conflicting interests. But since the boundaries of the *common* order are never finally settled (new interests forever create emergencies), since men disagree about what is private and public, political scientists have never been able to avoid deciding precisely what part of reality should be defined as political. Are the outbreaks of insurgents to be regarded as irrational convulsions or as political acts? Are budget bureaus, judicial tribunals, and corporate board meetings to be seen as political or nonpolitical institutions? Are the affairs of the Du Pont family private or public? Is the attempt to participate in public life a pathological reaction to private tensions or a healthy manifestation of a political impulse? Do so-called extremist movements provide relief for irrational drives or are they vehicles for dramatizing legitimate political values?

The answers to these questions will unavoidably depend on the political scientist's definition of politics. Initially his definition is of course likely to be derived from what he takes to be common knowledge of traditional ways of dealing with public affairs, from practices conventionally thought of as political. Yet political scientists do not necessarily accept given political institutions; they may decline to give accounts that merely serve to describe the structure and functions of existing systems. Whether or not they do will depend on their frame of mind. Inevitably, at least some of them will be moved to defy convention by accounting for phenomena not popularly regarded as political. Tired of articulating and refining political arrangements which are, so to speak, categorically established, they may seek to convey *their* findings in such a way as to widen the range of perceptions, offering reconstructions of what is widely assumed to be "natural" or "real" or "historically inevitable."

But whether political scientists choose to be conventional or not, their activities will be governed by their view of what aspects of human behavior it would be desirable to categorize as political. Their notion of what is desirable will elevate some parts of reality—and permit other parts to remain submerged, neg-

26

lected, and underprivileged. If, then, political scientists attempt to make some elements of reality coherent and significant, this is because they agree on what constitutes a note*worthy* state of affairs. Their attention is focused by their more or less implicit understanding of the meaning of such key terms as "politics," "citizen," "public," "participation," and "community." Mobilized and guided by a common paradigm, they are persuaded that they have identified the proper problems, know the proper procedures for verifying solutions, and use the proper symbols for communicating their knowledge.

III

The Cultivation of Reality

Prolonged fasting, ritualistic flagellation, and solemn exposure to sunlight piercing stained glass windows may have opened the door of perception for medieval monks, as Aldous Huxley has noted. Yet their testimony about the reality they beheld has no scientific standing today. Their alleged visions and findings remain suspect until science applies its procedure for gaining knowledge. Still, it is tempting simply to believe that intense devotion, enthusiasm, and rigor are sufficient to guarantee the validity of claims about what is really reality. One should like to agree with the contemporary physicist who insisted that adherence to the dictates of science means merely "doing your damndest—no holds barred." The motives which give rise to this disarming attitude—a desire for getting on with the job, an impatience with methodological polemics—certainly make it an appealing one. Who would not wish to believe that to enlarge the realm of knowledge, no procedure should be ruled out of order? Unavoidably, however, social scientists like everyone else do bar some holds in the effort to make experience manageable, to bring it under rational control. Some procedures—and not others—are regarded as irrelevant, uneconomical, inelegant, arbitrary, irresponsible, or bizarre.

That there may be various criteria for determining what validly constitutes knowledge and that all of them are subject to change is not always evident. Today, the underlying consensus on appropriate criteria which integrates the practices of American political science is so widespread that it easily appears as final. To be sure, a dogmatic posture is universally deplored as unscien-

tific. Academic courses would seem to exclude nothing sub-
human or superhuman; editors of scholarly journals in the discipline profess to be eclectic and permissive. What is more, there
are vigorous controversies about the merits of alternative analytical frameworks and research techniques. Yet if it were not for
a general agreement on professional norms it would be hard to
understand, for example, how graduate courses in scope and methods of political science can deal more lightly with scope than with
methods. Conflict assuredly takes place in political science, but
within boundaries so widely endorsed that their defenders perceive them as preordained, as virtually natural.

Thus if professional life is imaginative and competitive,
it is so within given boundaries. There are generous endorsements of new ventures, experimental probes, and innovative
approaches—endorsements readily given when it is felt that no
harm is likely to come to the discipline if one follows the advice
to do one's damndest, no holds barred. Such advice will be in-
terpreted to mean that one is to be "rigorous," "systematic,"
"exact," "disciplined," or simply "scientific." What *distinctive*
kind of "science" is to emerge needs scarcely to be specified explicitly: it is understood to be anything which can be established
within the frame accepted by political scientists—the frame
within which they identify problems, teach students, request
grants, conduct research, publish findings, and write texts. Just
as it is harmless to encourage well-schooled gentlemen to conduct themselves as they please, it is quite all right for contemporary political scientists to exhort one another to do their utmost.
Their professional activities will be no more unseemly than the
pleasures of the gentry; their freedom rests on constraints no less
pervasive for remaining unmentioned.

The lack of discussion of the qualities which distinguish
American political science makes it difficult for me to perceive its
dimensions and to become clear about possible alternative ways
of being scientific. This lack fosters the notion that at long last
political reality is being truly apprehended, that theology, metaphysics, parochialism, and sentimentality have been transcended,
and that the present paradigm merits exclusive respect. Were
prevailing practices discussed in terms which refer to their logical

30

and historical foundation, however, it would become easier to perceive the boundaries of political science. And were current commitments clearly specified, it would become apparent that there is life — even political life — beyond the boundaries, and that it may be mere convention which denies us access to it. Appreciation of these conventions should make it possible to entertain the belief that political science is in fact barring methods which might make more of our political experience comprehensible. By realizing that the freedom to participate in contemporary political science rests on prior constraints which are enforced by convention (or by conventional men with conventional interests), we may be able to enlarge the ground for action. We may be able to discern possibilities for political scientists to be differently constrained by a different discipline.

To outline unstated paradigmatic assumptions and to make them so explicit that they will reveal their distinctiveness, I should like sympathetically to identify with political scientists, understanding their work from their own point of view. Acting in their behalf, I should wish to treat their behavior as if it were all quite intentional. This involves seeing their work as they would see it if only they looked, and then spelling out its implications. The result is to establish a view from which it becomes possible to comprehend more than the practitioners of political science are prepared to acknowledge. It is to impute intentions and expand reality.[1]

The obvious objection to this procedure is that it leads to a fictitious, unverifiable view of the work done by contemporary political science. Does it not transform a welter of orientations and operations into a single school of thought? Does it not force individuals who argue with one another into unconscious alliance? A unified position is imputed, it will be said, to a highly variegated community of scholars — a position any one of its members might indignantly reject.

Yet I doubt that they would deny sharing at least some baseline. Even when contesting their findings, they would seem to understand one another, benefiting from the uniformity of introductory textbooks or the conventions of graduate curricula.[2] Moreover, unless certain assumptions and distinctions were com-

31

monly sustained, the work of political scientists would surely not make sense even to them: it would strike them as incoherent, contradictory, and finally meaningless.

Intellectual Foundations

Present-day political scientists may be concerned with the presuppositions of their activities, but not enough to do more than acknowledge turbulence and disaffection at the outer fringes of the profession. Sententious rhetoric combined with the promise of passable salaries has been sufficient to quiet dissidents. Dissidents are further accommodated in ways which make it possible to ignore them by offering them space within university departments, at academic conferences, in professional associations, or in scholarly journals. Tolerance prevails. There would appear to be no need for those engaged in teaching and research to probe the foundations of their work and contribute to the sociology of knowledge.

One way to make the ramifications of current work explicit is to place it in a larger context, to recover a past (or an unknown present) in which to see the emergence of the prevailing procedures, distinctions, and objectives. We can inquire how they made, how they *must* have made, their initial appearance. Because the innovators were under pressure to defend their new ventures, we should learn about presuppositions that remain unexpressed in current controversies.

But who are the innovators? Where should one locate the historical origins of contemporary political science? It has become conventional to review the history of political science as if the discipline were some recent invention. Its emergence is usually related in metaphors which dramatize a dialectical clash among protagonists who all happen to be twentieth-century Americans. The story of their scientific revolution is said to be uncomplicated and short. They have only recently fought for their respective positions, fighting to legitimate a focus first on institutions, then on groups, power, and decision-making, and finally on input-output systems — each successive position implying supposedly different postulates and raising supposedly different scientific problems. The assumption is that current work in the discipline

32

has confronted and overcome what are alleged to be radical differences. A newfound unity may be perceived; a new paradigm is said to be all but triumphant.[3]

But to see the limitations of these notions and recognize the shallowness of what are still believed to be fundamental clashes, I should like to expatriate myself and recall the voices of eighteenth-century innovators who argued against an opposition which was less tolerant and liberal than the exponents of American political science. Virtually all-embracing in their aims, these innovators were determined to capture not merely scientific enterprises but the whole of intellectual and artistic life. Emerging in the context of a fundamentally different tradition, they had to advance arguments which tended to reveal dimensions rarely exposed in modern times. As they battled to overcome what they believed to be widespread illusions and delusions, they were bound to be more thoroughgoing than American practitioners of political science. The innovators argued not for any specific research technique or analytical tool. Their concern, instead, was with making a totally new perspective plausible, with promoting a scientific revolution against what they claimed to be metaphysical excesses, willful ambiguities, elite-serving superstitions, prejudices, and ideologies. They established an entirely new vision; they both forced and freed men to see in a wholly new way.

The way was pioneered in the sciences by Francis Bacon's attack on a formidable armory of fetishes and fetters, on what he called the idols of the tribe, the cave, the market, and the theater. Human passions, traditions, and "the stageplays of philosophy," he said, block man's understanding of reality. But once these blocks have been removed, man will perceive nature's laws. Working within nature's laws and inducing nature to cooperate, man can put it to human use. As man progressively frees himself from theological and metaphysical dogma, he learns how to employ nature for his own ends. Knowing the causes of events, he has the power to produce desired effects.

Bacon, Kepler, Galileo, and Newton provided foundations that enabled the philosophers of the Enlightenment to argue for understanding observed phenomena wholly in terms of nature's laws. And these laws—both Galileo and Descartes ultimately made the point explicit—were basically written in the wholly

33

trustworthy language of mathematics. At bottom, beyond all appearance, the distinct components of the universe were to be comprehended in the indubitable terms of fixed mathematical relationships. These alone would relate the hard, distinct, immutable, tangible facts of experience to what Descartes called "clear and self-evident truths." Thus man could apprehend the order of the universe.

Distinguishing sharply between mind and body, Descartes proceeded to argue in favor of physiological explanations of human behavior. La Mettrie, building on Cartesian behavioral psychology, went further and identified man quite simply as machine. The whole of nature, he maintained, is best viewed mechanistically as a self-winding clock, each of its parts functional to the working of the whole. Man was finally to be known as an integrated component of larger systems, whether as a creature of his drives or as product of his social roles. Morality, theology, aesthetics, ultimately man's very dreams were to be comprehended in the objective, unambiguous terms of causal laws. As Hobbes was to put it in the seventeenth century, man's mind was best understood as "nothing but the motions in certain parts of an organic body." Given space and motion, everything might be explained. It became common to speak of both social mathematics (John de Witt) and social physics (Auguste Comte), with Comte providing the most concise program:

> We shall find that there is no chance of order and agreement but in subjecting social phenomena, like all others to invariable natural laws, which shall, as a whole, prescribe for each period, with entire certainty, the limits and character of political action: in other words, introducing into the study of social phenomena the same positive spirit which has regenerated every other branch of human speculation.[4]

The Ascendancy of Science

What began as an effort to establish scientific procedures for enhancing man's power over nature was ultimately to turn into a preoccupation with the procedures themselves. Initially, there seemed to be no point in asking for what ends man was to exercise power: knowing and mastering natural forces seemed a self-evident good. When twentieth-century scientists finally did feel the need to discriminate among conflicting ends and to implement some but not others, they—or at least their spokesmen—developed an attractive strategy. They distinguished between their roles as scientists concerned with procedures and their roles as citizens concerned with the wisdom of alternative policies. They could presume to be knowledgeable and discriminating about means, not ends. They conceded that, as scientists, they were not competent to judge matters for which the rational methods of science were inappropriate. They could describe, not prescribe. They could operate effectively in the objective domain of science, but they would have to be silent or speak without authority in the subjective domain of human values.

While this posture implied an appealing modesty, it freed scientists to work more energetically and purposefully on techniques for extending man's power. Having no conception of science itself as a social movement, scientists could treat politics as a mere avocation. They found it all the more easy to disregard the purposes of a wider community because liberalism offered no community theory in any case—nothing to frame the ends of political action, to identify the public interest, to define a just society. Dismissing critics who noted that the enterprise of science was bedeviled by compulsive innovation and growth addiction, that it neglected constraints which make *continuous* human activity possible, scientists could concentrate on doing science. Involved in observing, comparing, and experimenting, they assuredly succeeded in adding to the body of empirically confirmed propositions. Whatever diverse ends men might seek privately or as socially responsible citizens, the end of science at least was to subject nature to rational control. And insofar as "rational" meant "scientific" there was properly no end for science which science itself did not set. Science would ideally be subjected to its own canons, not to canons dictated by outsiders. What constituted "rational" control was to be derived from the conventions of science itself. Thus science, setting its own goals, could, in a word, he regarded as an autonomous activity.

There could hardly be any effective challenge to this development. Above all, the scientific way of proceeding assuredly *worked:* it elaborately displayed the beneficial effects so widely claimed for it. Moreover, the techniques of science were no secret; they could be employed by anyone who liked to solve puzzles and was determined to make a name for himself. The scientific community was open to men who might be excluded from religious orders, high society, monarchical regimes, and aristocratic classes. More than that, science could focus on society and be used, as Machiavelli saw, to unmask rulers who exercised power selfishly. The mass of men manipulated by ideologies which had reinforced royal estates, the priesthood, and economic monopolies could be emancipated by a social science determined to expose the unempirical character of prerevolutionary dogma. The appeal of a science at once democratic, effective, and liberating was virtually irresistible.

The possibility that social science, like all science, might set its own ends — or that it might permit its means to be treated as ends — could scarcely be perceived as a threat to man's integrity, and even less as a threat to his survival. That it seemed unnecessary to be troubled by the ends of science, that it became respect-

> *All statistics, all work that is merely descriptive or informative, imply the ambitious and perhaps groundless hope that in the incalculable future men like us, but with clearer minds, will infer from the data that we leave them some useful conclusion or some hidden truth.*
>
> —Jorge Luis Borges
> "An Evening with Ramón Bonavena" (1970)

able to become wholly absorbed by science itself, is thus readily understandable.

Even so, the innovators themselves had never been without misgivings. Bacon, for instance, had no doubts about the positive value of nonscientific, religious enterprises; he expected science to vindicate the divine order of things. Further, he feared that the very idols which science would destroy might ultimately be reinstated in the scientific community itself "unless mankind when forewarned guard themselves with all possible care against them."[5] Descartes, too, was far from eliminating an independent, subjective element from the quest for certain knowledge; determined to give new stature to man's mind, he explicitly included accounts of his perception of himself—his own goals—in his *Discourse on Method*. And Hobbes had stipulated an ideal for which empirical science itself could provide no warrant: the individual's existential footing. He sought to free men from those metaphysical notions which had inhibited their development and kept them from asserting themselves.

Mandates for Political Science

Whatever contributed to making physical science a spectacular practical success—adherence to agreed-on procedures, the inspired hunches of individual creators, openness to new talent, the way material rewards gave impetus to the quest for more material rewards—scientific enterprises were guided by directives attractive to social scientists interested in the workings of society. If the physical universe could be rationally governed by the impersonal force of science, why not the human universe?

Not surprisingly, the ideas sustaining the physical sciences appeared to hold out great promise to students of society and politics. This was less because the actual operations of physical science were understood[6] than because physical science had achieved immense prestige for solving practical problems even while pursuing its own ends. By the middle of the twentieth century there was certainly good reason for thinking that the social sciences might do as well: their subject matter was becoming increasingly suitable for the approaches and methods of physical science. The historical trends associated with technological development—especially urbanization—generated social routines that neatly lend themselves to empirical scrutiny and statistical analysis. Furthermore, the game scientists play promised intellectual excitement and aesthetic pleasure. But perhaps most basically the appeal of the physical sciences to outsiders was due to a longing for tidiness and unity, an interest in recovering an authoritative order for social life after the upheavals of the French and the Industrial revolutions. Reactionary or not, it was tempting to assume that the whole of reality is a vast, unbroken continuum and that the workings of its constitutive elements must therefore be expressible in a single language. Physicists, willingly speaking as philosophers, certainly gave credence to this assumption. Galileo had been only the first to note that

> *Philosophy is written in that vast book which stands ever open before our eyes, I mean the universe; but it cannot be read until we have learnt the language and become familiar with the characters in which it is written. It is written in mathematical language, and the letters are triangles, circles and other geometrical figures, without which means it is humanly impossible to comprehend a single word.*[7]

Ultimately, the problem for students of politics was to decipher the political universe by somehow joining with scientists in all fields, to become truly interdisciplinary, and to learn the language of mathematics. To be sure, it was always urged that one might still appreciate the "insights" buried in work others had not pursued in a truly scientific spirit, that the unification of political science should not be attempted prematurely, that the first steps toward an integrated science be taken cautiously, and that one must certainly avoid—in a phrase that was to become a cliché— the slavish imitation of the physical sciences. Yet the fundamental directives seem to me increasingly clear:

1. *Let convention define the basic units of political analysis.* Common sense and ordinary language should identify the boundaries of the central concepts of political science, determining the meaning of such terms as "behavior," "interest," "individual," "nation," "public," "event," and "political." "Politics," for example, should be defined in conventional terms as essentially the activity of people seeking to get or keep power so as to gain personal rewards.

2. *Assume that the subject matter of political science— data regarded as distinctively political—is basically invariable and unequivocal.* The focus of political science should be on political relationships which are in principle unambiguously specifiable.

3. *Approach the world of politics as if it were so constituted that the patterns inherent within it are observable.* Political life lends itself to observation, being composed of "hard" and "visible" slices of reality. Although there are also such "soft" phenomena as values, intentions, thoughts, and moods, these are necessarily ambiguous and therefore not eligible as such for inclusion in a framework of concepts—not until political science has either transformed them experimentally into unambiguous data or reduced them analytically to an unambiguous substructure of concepts.

4. *Test propositions about individuals and groups in politics by controlled observation of overt behavior over time.* Observation, which means looking at the plain facts with the aid of hypotheses or attention-directing models, yields findings.[8] The validity of specific propositions or general theories should be tested against the evidence "out there"; evidence alone can falsify what is untenable and establish what survives testing. Inductive reasoning from facts to generalizations serves to confirm and accumulate knowledge of relevant reality. Erroneous conclusions are progressively eliminated as reality is more clearly and precisely apprehended.

5. *Treat the world of politics as a functional system.* By assuming the existence of recurrent elements of political reality, one can locate the regularities, patterns, and uniformities which are characteristic of ongoing systems. General theories—when empirically supported by investigations disclosing the underlying immutable, invariable determinants of behavior—describe how the elements of political reality are functionally related, each contributing to the maintenance of the whole.

6. *Define men as individuals whose conduct—whose movement in time and space—is the product of tangible forces.* Human behavior should be understood in terms of biological, physical, economic, psychological, or social systems within which the individual can be seen to function, being driven to seek approval, maximize utilities, and acquire power over scarce resources.

7. *Understand the world of politics by seeking to uncover the causes of events or by specifying the conditions under which they occur.* An ordering of events which shows them either to be

probable results of prior events or to have occurred under variable conditions provides the most acceptable kind of explanation.

8. *State explanations in terms of conclusions drawn from the relevant evidence.* Explanations should be seen as the end product of inquiry, that is, as findings that settle previously unsettled issues.

9. *Express propositions—entire theories—in as unambiguous terms as possible.* To facilitate communication, theories should be carefully expressed in language others cannot misunderstand. Purged of equivocal meanings, the elements of theories

> *Come clean.*
>
> —American colloquialism

will correspond to the equally unequivocal elements of reality. Theories are thus objective. The observer's subjective values, interests, or intentions generate research and define its range; but they have no legitimate place in scientific formulations. The purest, most rigorous language being that of mathematics, theories are best expressed in impersonal, quantitative terms.

10. *Develop the tools, methods, measures, and instruments which facilitate observation and lead to increasingly less ambiguous formulations of its results.*

11. *Work on problems which are set by scientific theory.* The agenda of relevant questions for research should be derived from the welter of troublesome inconsistencies, gaps, and anomalies revealed by prevailing theory.

12. *Be alert to whatever clues for theory construction are implicit in neighboring disciplines.* Since the limits of political science are set not by disciplinary labels but by the tenets of science, one should always be receptive to the scientific work pursued by sociologists, anthropologists, psychologists, economists, and even some historians, welcoming them as potential or actual collaborators.

By providing this neat enumeration of directives, intimating that precisely twelve are distinguishable, I am of course ignoring the subtle, complex ways all of them are tangled in practice. Certainly they do not emerge this nicely from the operations of political science.[9] Like all abstractions, they (and whoever makes them up) are put to shame by a far richer reality. In fact, I know few political scientists who would wish to claim that in their search for an autonomous reality, they actually care to remain detached from their data and to be formalistic in the presentation of their findings. Although they may recognize their discipline's directives in principle, they do not necessarily live up to their pledge. As they betray their own paradigmatic ideals, they often show themselves to be more attracted by an exciting process of research than by the mandate to formulate its end results. They may even allow that their work did not amount to much, that their conclusions are banal, really pleas for more research and money to support it—as if the research process might be rewarding enough by itself. Digressing and deviating, sacrificing rigor and risking loss of support, researchers may permit themselves an occasional idiosyncratic insight; or they may end on an evocative note of intriguing ambiguity rather than with the precise denotative phrase. Nevertheless, they would feel obliged to acknowledge that such behavior is an undisciplined, self-indulgent failing, permissible only when relegated to footnotes, confined to acknowledgments, or popularized in nonprofessional magazines.

To remain disciplined, the political scientist must in any case act in accordance with the prevailing norms of scientific research. These alone can make him attend to political life as it "really" is—a persistent, inherently meaningful composite of decisions made, of policies adopted and governments established, of bargains struck, victories won, and boundaries settled. Having come within his range of vision and having been caught within his conceptual nets, these manifest aspects of reality must be carefully articulated, related to one another, and finally expressed in the form of generalizations. Thus is reality confirmed.

The Uses of Rigor

To enter and make his way within his professional community—to be rewarded by it—the political scientist will understandably conform to its central directives. His work will otherwise be regarded as wasteful and frivolous, as unprofessional and unsystematic, in any event as unrewarding. It will be said (or vaguely felt) to lack rigor and precision, and hence to fall outside the system of science. Accordingly, he will feel prompted to respect the currently prevailing norms and permit them to give his own enterprise its specific structure and orientation. He will be impelled to commit himself—even if not consistently—to the battery of generally endorsed distinctions:

objective fact/subjective value
description/prescription
theory/practice
value-neutral means/value-permeated ends
impersonal detachment/personal involvement
behavior/action
public knowledge/private opinion
the knowing scholar/the known subject matter
scientist/citizen

Ordering the life of political scientists, these distinctions constitute, as it were, a prescriptive grammar, one which indicates which expressions and modes of behavior are appropriate to scientific operations. This grammar dictates the proper literary style, determines the content of publications, and articulates the practical roles to to be played. Basically, it defines what it really *means* to be a political scientist. Insofar as it maintains the scientific goal of neutrality, it divorces the order of science from that of private opinion, subjective interest, and personal choice.

Obvious if not always noted advantages derive from a commitment to the distinctions between objective description and subjective prescription, between fact and norm, between the knower and the known, and between the role of scientist and that of citizen. As political scientists put private valuations, interests, and preferences to the side, they are more able to concentrate their energies and give their scientific work literally undivided attention. Making values and merely personal convictions extraneous to the scientific process of validation, they increasingly free themselves (at least in their role as scientists) from those metaphysical distractions—those exuberant outbursts—which keep distorting human knowledge. Because they can agree on a fundamentally decisive criterion of truth – immediate sense experience as linked with theories by chains of explicative definitions – they are able to rely on this consensus to overcome private interest and local prejudice. Their collective effort to validate hypotheses so as to contribute to shared scientific knowledge enables them to eliminate idiosyncrasies of manner or style. Organized under the banner of objectivity, they are the beneficiaries of a professional movement which bestows status and offers meaningful employment. To the extent that scientifically investigated experience is referred to a common, professionally accepted "frame of reference," there is the inspiring promise of the integration of dispersed research projects, of knowledge unified at last.

Having reacted to a crude, fact-infatuated empiricism, political scientists are reaching for comprehensive theory, for broad-gauge generalizations, for conceptual nets of interrelated categories. What the theory is expected to frame is the universally experienced substance of politics – political reality. Defining the range of political phenomena – of political man, political action, and political systems – a unified theory will ideally specify which facts are the relevant ones. Thus the very definition of political experience that an authentic empiricism must continuously challenge is settled at the outset by the accepted analytical framework. The underlying issue being settled a priori, work can commence in earnest.

Insofar as a common frame of reference comes to constitute the coherent basis for large-scale enterprises, it has the virtue of facilitating the classification and placement of specialized talent. It promotes teamwork and a sense of loyalty. Further, the initial agreement on what politics "really" is, an agreement which conveniently secures the foundation of research, helps to make scientific work attractive to individuals who are disconcerted by the ambiguities of speech and politics, by procedures which impel the *continuous* identification and evaluation of one's interests. Such a constitution for science fulfills at least one of Bacon's great hopes:

> *The course I propose for the discovery of science is such as leaves but little to the acuteness and strength of wits, but*

places all wits and understandings nearly on a level. For
as in the drawing of a straight line or a perfect circle,
much depends on the steadiness and practice of the hand,
if it be done by aim of hand only, but if with the aid of rule
or compass, little or nothing; so it is exactly with my plan.[10]

As the discipline becomes technical, those who find technical
work congenial—those who enjoy what Kuhn has called puzzle-
solving—should be attracted and rewarded. This does not mean
new recruits are necessarily ignorant of their own political interests or devoid of moral sensibilities; it merely means that they
can keep their politics divorced from their work, that on the one
hand they can value the objective realm of science and on the
other the subjective one of politics. Such economizing is apt to
lead to greater scientific productivity while it reduces professional conflict and maintains individual morale.

Not surprisingly, I find the less dramatic, more ambiguous
results of entertaining the existing paradigmatic distinctions con-
siderably harder to outline and appreciate.[11] What is *not* done (or
done confusingly) is in any case more difficult to define. Thus as
political scientists distinguish between an impersonal realm of
facts and a personal one of values—and as they professionally discriminate against the latter—they keep part of themselves out of
their work and avoid articulating their own quite special interests,

> *In relation to their systems, most systematizers*
> *are like a man who builds an enormous castle*
> *and lives in a shack beside it; they do not*
> *live in their own enormous systematic buildings.*
> *but spiritually speaking a man's thought must*
> *be the building in which he lives—otherwise*
> *everything is inverted.*
>
> —Søren Kierkegaard
> "Journal," February 7, 1846

even when these might give life and color to their enterprises. As
authors, they remain aloof from their field and alienated from their
prose, nonparticipants in the name of science. True, they readily

44

affirm their personal concern for the disinterested pursuit of truth. Moreover, they follow what has become solemn convention and note their devotion to human dignity, peace, freedom, justice, development, democracy, welfare, and clean air. But their amorphous declarations hardly serve to delimit the goals of research. In practice, research is neither aimless nor arbitrary: it is delimited by those who design it, authors who are present, however concealed. Just as likely—especially when the author makes every effort to be self-effacing—the work is given direction by the prevailing winds of doctrine, the ideology of the day, the mood of the time, or by those who set the mood, those in society empowered to formulate goals and define problems in relation to them. Since the projects of political science are unavoidably limited, since values, interests, and purposes direct and permeate all human enterprises, the question cannot be whether values (or biases) are to be admitted but rather which ones to admit.

Remaining silent about the *specific* goals of research is by no means inconvenient, for it saves the political scientist from having to engage in transactions with himself or his world. He need not identify his concerns or explicitly avow consensually held beliefs. If he professes, for instance, to be involved in peace research, he may conveniently understand "peace" as what is generally so regarded—that is, as a condition acceptable to those who have the power to shape opinion. He can think of peace simply as well-managed conflict among nations, as an arrangement for preventing the emergence of a new state of affairs disturbing to dominant groups. Opposed to "war," he can quite naturally turn out to favor not the repression of all men inclined to violence—rulers as well as ruled—but the repression of the ruled. Treating the acts of the rulers as if they were lawful, he can view the behavior of the ruled as lawless. Insofar as his inarticulate convictions and attitudes simply conform to the dominant ideology, the range and direction of his research are set. The dominant ideology will provide him with such presumably stable units of analysis as "nation," "group," "decision," or "system." And since his operations will not disturb reality—are designed not to interfere—he will discover and report on those aspects of reality which are sufficiently well established to make themselves known to him. Sensitive to men, movements, and behavior patterns which are persistent, accredited, privileged, respected, articulate, coherent, organized, effective, and potent—looking for what he believes is only natural—he cannot avoid finding phenomena characterized by such estimable qualities. *Some* things "out there" will assuredly turn out to look durable and therefore notable. They will seem to be indubitably real. He will be struck by them, for his research design welcomes and arms them. Other patterns are admittedly present; but they are seen to be in a state of disarray—a state which he may be moved to "explain" not by revealing their meaning but by specifying the conditions which bring them about.

Unencumbered by the need to specify his interests as he seeks to take account of reality—or specifying his interests only in the broadest of terms—he accommodates interests which are established. He is led to accept the very definition of "relevance" and "significance" which constitutes the ideology of the day; he embraces the prevailing beliefs about what properly constitutes politics, order, lawfulness, peace, or justice. These beliefs, not surprisingly, are precisely the ideology of those who reward him—public agencies, private foundations, or senior professional colleagues. Declining to play the role of citizen when doing science, he implicitly accepts the decisions of those who have the power to make political choices, who decide the major issues of war and peace, define law and order, and specify what policies properly constitute welfare, recreation, health, education, or communication.

This ideological conformity need not mean that his science will necessarily compromise his personal convictions, for as citizen he may be no less inclined to endorse the policies upheld by the powerful. Not suffering from role strain, he then scarcely feels troubled as he seeks to put the dominant ideology to scientific tests, inquiring how we can "make democracy work" or how we can "bring peace to nations" or how we can "reduce violence in inner-city ghettos." Finding answers, he then welcomes whatever agencies may implement his "solutions." Thus the distinctions between the role of citizen and scientist, between political ideals and political reality turn out to be as pleasing to live with as they are easy to proclaim. In practice these distinctions lose significance.

Geared to a settled, predefined political reality, *trusting* it, political science remains on the side of its triumphant—or at

46

least surviving—elements. Political science gives credible explanations of the way prevailing systems and privileged organizations function, of their capacity to adapt to emergencies and meet crises. Publicizing its findings, it is part of the social process, implicated in public policy. Its practitioners, not disposed to interfere with established reality from the outside, perceiving such transactions as unscientific, readily make the prevailing problems of society those of science. It becomes the proper task of such a science to search for the type of instrumental knowledge useful for governing men within the existing political order, for integrating them in established systems while instructing them which of their experiences they are to accept as part of political reality and which they must dismiss as unreal, private, and disreputable. Perhaps it will yet become possible to look back on such a political science the way Hannah Arendt has looked back on those who in the late 1960s lied for their country from within the walls of the Pentagon:

> *They obviously were different from the ordinary image makers. Their distinction lies in that they were problem-solvers as well, hence they were not just intelligent but prided themselves on being "rational," and they were indeed to a rather frightening degree above "sentimentality" and in love with "theory," the world of sheer mental effort. They were eager to find formulae, preferably expressed in a pseudo-mathematical language, which would unify the most disparate phenomena with which reality presented them, that is, they were eager to discover laws by which to explain and predict political and historical facts as though they were as necessary, and thus as reliable, as the physicists once believed natural phenomena to be.*[12]

47

IV
The Recovery of Experience

Whatever the ambitions of contemporary political science, little is actually claimed for the way the results of research have enriched understanding of political processes or extended our ability to govern ourselves. There is much hope, but admittedly only a modest yield in useful conclusions. Yet the discipline is not without its attractions. After all, the various kinds of research popular today do provide opportunities for participation in complex activities, encouraging the display of talent and industriousness. This opportunity to participate in a community of scholars is no small reward, especially since the promise is held out that, however little is known today, ultimately more of consequence will be learned about the operations of various political systems, the techniques for managing conflict, and the priorities for further national development. What political scientists now know only vaguely and in ways not yet directly applicable they may yet learn to make increasingly precise and useful. And in the meantime, they can find themselves involved in inherently gratifying research.

Despite these wholesome developments, doubts continue to be raised about the rewards of working within the discipline. Even those who readily accept the prevailing paradigm and engage in what Thomas Kuhn has called normal science have felt impelled to note that not all is well. In fact, there is not only the usual readiness to expose technical errors but also an emerging disposition to question the very assumptions which underlie current professional activities.

The Troubled Profession

It is no longer hard to see the reasons for the dissatisfactions near the outer edge of the discipline. What has become disquieting is the profession's reluctance — or inability — to frame and illuminate the major events of recent times, events which, because they were so unexpected, are widely seen as constituting a state of crisis. The contemporary crisis in authority — to reduce the contemporary situation to too simple a denominator — did find expression in the outcries of prophets, seers, mystics, preachers, and assorted metaphysicians. It also found expression in the work of novelists, playwrights, film directors, poets, and maverick social scientists such as Jules Henry, Erich Fromm, Herbert Marcuse, and C. Wright Mills. Yet despite the thrust of the work of these various critics, there seemed to be no way for political scientists to give it recognition. When reviewed at all, their work was characterized as nonprofessional, as "merely" insightful, brilliant, and intuitive, but not as disciplined effort to bring politically relevant feelings under control. Only retrospectively has it seemed possible to give credit to ostensibly undisciplined writers, to appreciate unconventional approaches for managing the discontents of the modern world.

In any case, political scientists have scarcely subjected our incapacity to govern ourselves — to control the most brutal and the most generous of our impulses at home and abroad — to disciplined statement. Critics of the profession have not had to go apocalyptic and turn to the major catastrophes of the age to become disconcerted about the way professional activities have remained unrelated to moral sensibilities. Close at hand in seemingly unimportant sectors of our lives there has been enough trouble to raise questions about the direction and presuppositions of political science as a collective activity: unseen parts of the body politic have made themselves visible. Suddenly pushing their own way into camera range, previously unrecognized and unrepresented men have fought to be perceived as significant, to be named and counted, literally to register as voters, as men who mattered and whose autobiographies were worthy of note. If they have not been seen as significant by a political science which at best took account of them as forces which reacted and not as men who resolved to act, they have certainly compelled administrators and legislators to become alert. Submerged groups (students, women, blacks, prisoners, stockholders, deputy sheriffs, construction workers, civil servants, and even Army recruits, though not yet patients, teachers, or coal miners) have crashed into the mass media and from there into the courts, legislatures, and administrative agencies.

Their emergence (inevitably characterized as an emergency by those within the consensus) could of course be made comprehensible enough by political science. For example, the specification of such preconditions of riots as long hot summers, economic deprivation, or a sense of powerlessness could lead to more precise predictions. Knowledge of the causes of violence among groups or nations could make forecasts of its incidence increasingly accurate.

But while causal analysis could allow political science to cope with newly emerging data, the offered explanations still have not pacified the critics within the profession: subjects attended to and illuminated by artists, journalists, novelists, and film directors have become part of public life even while such subjects continued to elude the framework of political science. Scientifically accredited approaches to understanding have sought to reach the new politics — but succeeded in grasping little of consequence. True, individuals have been seen in motion — but merely as reflexes and outputs, as dependent variables, as effects of causes. Whereas political scientists might have been privately convinced that people should be respected as agents who engage in meaningful action, professionally they have accounted for little which exhibits purpose, meaning, dignity, or integrity.

Not surprisingly, the various new forms of behavior ranging from insurgencies abroad to riots at home have been seen as counterproductive, as manifestly dysfunctional. Acting professionally, political scientists have perceived manipulated and manipulatable data. But as men with larger concerns and a greater range of compassion than allowed by their profession, they have also perceived something else—namely the public significance of others who happen to make their own way outside the explicitly acknowledged balance of interests. Identifying science with the findings embodied in positivist theory, believing explanations to be unambiguous generalizations about neatly assorted variables, political scientists have remained professionally insensitive to the specific contexts which give meaning to human action. As nonprofessionals, however, they have been sensitive precisely to such contexts, perceiving that the astringency of their paradigm has kept them from recognizing new meanings.

In other words, by the 1960s previously unrecognized individuals and groups had appeared in plain view of others. But from within the confines of political science they continued to seem somehow "unreal"—*and this despite the fact that their appearance begged for recognition.* Realizing what they were missing and how their feelings—their mere feelings—were being systematically betrayed by the self-imposed paradigmatic limits of their discipline, at least some political scientists could not help but inquire what could be done. If the dominant commitment to the surface facts of politics was so disconcerting, what might be the alternative? Could one find a basis in logic or experience for alternative assumptions, procedures, tools, and activities? Where might one search for a new foundation? How might the domain of political science be expanded so as to make more of our political experience comprehensible? Could the profession be less ungenerous?

In probing for answers, political scientists have acted like other men in similar circumstances: they have been somewhat less inclined to challenge their axiomatic assumptions than to work on improving familiar methods. They have persisted in operating within the existing framework—often with new zeal and ingenuity. If they have found their science to be stultifying, they have also believed that only their science—and a few new extracurricular activities—can liberate. Their science will provide increasingly serviceable explanations, better solutions to nontrivial problems, more useful findings. Once duly policy oriented —relevant to the political needs of the day—their science will yield discoveries which can be put to practical use.

The very strenuousness of this drive for relevant and useful answers has made it especially difficult to keep in mind that political science — indeed, all the sciences, all the humanities, man's projects generally — are motivated by a concern for something more than end results, that their point is not only to bring things to conclusions. Like the performances of dancers or athletes or politicians, those of political scientists may also be seen as efforts to provide participants with opportunities for testing themselves in relation to accepted rules — regardless of outcomes. How the game is played, with what measure of grace and economy of motion, matters no less than some ultimate payoff. Moreover, political scientists may also acknowledge their concern with so revising the rules of their game that it will manage to hold the attention of those moved to participate in it. They may see themselves as defining problems and designing ways for meeting them. "Men did not begin to shoot because there were ready-made targets to aim at," John Dewey observed; "they made things into targets by shooting at them, and then made special targets to make shooting more significantly interesting." For men who live above a mere subsistence level, *relevant* problems are no more simply "given" than *relevant* facts. When men are free to define relevancy, when their roles are not dictated by social structures, neither problems nor facts should be treated as somehow preestablished or ready-made by nature. In the world of culture — whether it is the culture of politics or of science — men themselves define relevancy. Problems and facts are but human constructions; their creation is a characteristically humanistic activity.[1] Whenever the conventional range of problems (and hence the conventional order of facts) fails to be *interesting*, men feel quite naturally moved to raise new problems which create a new order of facts and establish new relationships.

That it is quite natural for men to play this creative role is not always evident, for the opportunity to define "relevancy" is not always present. All too often, it is imperative simply to try to keep alive. When survival is threatened, when unquestionably serious matters of life and death keep men from imagining alternatives, they live involuntarily. Using what knowledge they have, they are then *determined* to apply it without fuss or doubt. Facing such indubitable threats to life as epidemics or floods, they will of course resent the inconclusive games that scientists and scholars like to play. Yet once men find relief from the kind of pressure which makes animals of us all by depriving us of the time and security to doubt and reflect, they will once again turn to characteristically human enterprises. They will then engage in sports, games, and politics, become participants in the sciences and the arts—the various enterprises of culture. This humanistic, cultural quality of life becomes evident insofar as men act rather than react, insofar as they have escaped necessity and are consequently free to create options, free to divert themselves by designing "special targets to make shooting more significantly interesting."

Kept from engaging in this humanistic activity, men remain arrested wherever they happen to be, locked into currently established institutions. To continuously enlarge the focus of the arts and the sciences, it should therefore be helpful to remind ourselves how men have found time—or taken time out—to experiment, probe, and play, how they have sought to express themselves by giving vent to their natural sense of curiosity, their romantic impulse to treat the present—the here and now—as incomplete.

To succeed in their efforts to master the unknown and make it familiar, men have had to resolve not to treat either themselves or any prevailing reality with full seriousness. Whether they have acted as politicians, scientists, or artists, they have had to treat every convention as partial—and all who consent to it as partisans. Even while respected for being in command of the procedures and the knowledge of their discipline, they have had to be ready to put both in jeopardy, ready to violate the very etiquette which prescribed how The Compleat Politician or The True Scientist or The Ideal Artist is to behave. What their predecessors claim to have confirmed, they have had to regard as mere hypotheses.[2]

There is no reason for the political scientist to aspire to less. Why should he not treat himself as if he, too, were involved in the human enterprise? To break his self-imposed professional ties—his comforting connections—he, too, must welcome whatever might bring more of reality into what he calls his professional life. Accordingly, he must conceive of his enterprise as not readily distinguishable from *any* human discipline, from *any* effort to bestow meaning on our inexplicable existence. He must risk losing his home and his identity, not be ashamed to appear as a human being expressing human interests. He must let his work be less special and precious as it becomes more open to general public concerns. His life will be fuller and less stable as he becomes skeptical not only about his present accumulation of scientific findings but also about the set of fixations and conventions which have so far served to give him a living wage, regular hours, and office furniture.

Foundations For Creativity

Because such skepticism works against efforts to overcome uncertainties and solve problems, it is hard to make it attractive in practice. There always seems to be good reason for putting an end to the dynamism, the endless creativity, entailed by a commitment to skepticism. Still, I think it is possible to give weight and authority to the turbulence engendered by skepticism: political scientists—like all of us—may maintain their composure to the extent that they succeed in detaching themselves from specific, immediate interests—problems that seemingly must be solved—and locate some distant or more generalized ground for the freedom to remain inconclusively in action. A review of previous attempts to elucidate a commitment to remaining rebellious, creative, playful, and political may serve to legitimize it today at least for those who can afford to treat their life as less than real and the future as less than fixed. Moreover, such a review may show how little political scientists have exercised their warrant for creativity, for making private experiences public. They may come to see themselves as needlessly constrained—constrained not only by the inexorable forces of physical and biological nature but also by their intellectual conventions or ideological commitments. A survey of the philosophical ground which Machiavelli, Hobbes, Kant, Nietzsche, and others have provided should disclose opportunities for public action that political scientists conceal from themselves even as they proclaim themselves to be in action.

There is a further reason for recalling the past. The fact that writers such as Kant expressed themselves in an idiom which is not altogether ours should paradoxically make it easier to accept them in all their dimensions—not only in ways that happen to be convenient. Translating an unfamiliar idiom, the political scientist is compelled to think along with these writers; by the time he works his way into the ramifications of their work, his own defenses should be down. Making the past present to himself, he may be more able to abandon some of his current commitments.

It should be useful, in my view, to begin with Machiavelli and recall the implications of his effort to take his bearings not by a timeless morality but by man's need to fortify that common order which man requires to maintain himself in the face of pervasive political instability. Disdaining abstractions unrelated to human needs, Machiavelli found it easy to appreciate the virtuosity of statesmen, to treat mere appearances as significant, and to attend as fully as he could to the politics of this world. In the management of our secular affairs, so he showed at length, we cannot avoid deception and casuistry, dissembling and opportunism: in practice some interest (and some moral principle designed to rationalize it) must always be violated to accommodate another interest. In public life, vice turns into virtue, evil into good. Political history is radically ambiguous, permeated by irony. To govern, the ruler must therefore "have a mind disposed to adapt itself according to the wind, and as the variations of fortune dictate."[3] Disregarding abstract principles, Machiavelli's new science respected the infinitely flexible ways in which the powerful could maneuver to cope with their environment. He sought to show how creatively the environment could be managed to maintain political arenas, how life could be governed not by chance or nature but by the interests of men.

Machiavelli's steady focus on the needs of men as he prescribed prudential rules of conduct was intensified in the ethics of Spinoza as well as in the work of Hobbes. Hobbes especially saw individuals obligated to become so self-regarding that he made skepticism toward everything we have not created by ourselves into a universal epistemological imperative: we can only know, he reasoned, what we have made. It was Kant, however, who opened the way for a skeptical posture that served as the great liberator of our creative impulses. He sought to free the individual from all but what he called categorical imperatives, contending (like Rousseau) that we can have full confidence only in laws to which we ourselves have given consent. Prior to Kant, man as creative being designing his own laws, as protean artist, had been constrained: he was assigned the unobtrusive role of illuminating the nature of things. The various expressions of what man beheld, his works of art, were merely to reflect an inherently orderly reality. They were to celebrate and intensify reality, disclosing its ideal qualities. One had merely to hold a polished mirror up to nature to reveal its inner harmony. Kant's *Critique of Pure Reason*, however, argued that whatever normative order might inhere in the universe, it would surely not disclose itself. About the "nature" of "reality," we could no longer presume to say anything conclusively true. We would have to remain equivocal, make only questionable statements, and put these to the test in practice. Nature—or rather what those in power asserted to be nature—might now yield to men prepared to test hypotheses, that is, to men in action. If the natural world was to be increasingly humanized, it had to be transformed. Individuals were thus summoned to establish themselves, to make whatever laws, formulas, myths, designs, languages, and ideologies satisfied their needs. They could ignore demands not related to their needs, learning how needlessly they were constrained by fixations they falsely believed to be objectively true.

Kant (anticipated in this by Rousseau) authorized men to appropriate what was called reality, to structure their own experiences, to give form to their lives—in sum, to express themselves. Thus they would cease to be victimized by need-frustrating elites and languages, cease to be consumed by the forces of nature and slowly commence (in Antonin Artaud's phrase) to *signal* through the flames.

To be sure, men had affirmed themselves and rebelled against necessity from the time they first appeared on the historical stage. But it had always been difficult to perceive and respect their behavior as expressive. What evidence could be found for what was not clearly evident to the senses? When men have been observed in motion, what usually seemed manifest was their powerlessness, the dominance of their drives, the primacy of pressures, forces, and conditions they could not control. One could certainly not *see* men as conscious of their experience, as motivated to surmount their fate whether by scorning it (like Camus's Sisyphus) or by deliberately signaling (like Artaud's unhysterical Joan of Arc at the stake) — thus remaining in charge and composed, refusing to tremble in uncontrolled panic. But once this invisible, willful determination to govern oneself in clear view of others was postulated, men could be seen as resolved not only to endure but also to remain known to the community of the living, to keep relating to one another even at the end and near despair. Even when too exhausted to speak up, they could yet be seen *willing* to proclaim that they were struggling to confer meaning on part of the world, doing what they could so as to make even the most painful part distinctively human, an extension of the range of human concerns, a refinement of the experience of man.

Of course it is also possible — *desirable,* Schopenhauer argued in the nineteenth century — to intensify one's experience by proceeding to extinguish impulses which contribute to one's will to live: a disciplined asceticism and finally self-annihilation through either suicide or mysticism is a way out of this world

> *Everything which comes into existence proves precisely by coming into existence that it is not necessary, for the only thing which cannot come into existence is the necessary, because the necessary is.*
>
> — Søren Kierkegaard
> "Philosophical Fragments" (1962)

when we are persuaded that no tokens, gestures, signs, icons, emblems, myths, religions, or metaphysics can ultimately console us and give meaning to our existence. Schopenhauer saw symbolic forms as but expressions of our absurd will to live, that is, to suffer. To escape life's pain and anguish — including the ultimately futile labor of constructing consoling rituals and symbol systems — we are morally obliged to negate life itself. Acts of negation alone were justifiable.

Placing Forms in Open Space

Schopenhauer's view of the world as devoid of intrinsic significance and of man as incapable of deriving any moral justification for his life from the order of the universe was to be wholly accepted by Nietzsche. But Nietzsche discerned that Schopenhauer had not wholly dispensed with at least one abstract, culture-bound moral justification: Schopenhauer's life-denying pessimism had been derived from an autonomous morality of compassion, an unwarranted identification of amoral life with immoral suffering. Nietzsche, too, saw the world as sheer "will and representation"; he, too, saw humanity existing in a godless universe holding nothing of significance except such "representations" as man can make significant by the exercise of his powers. But he assented to the *whole* of life, including those painful aspects of it which Schopenhauer felt to be the worst. He sought desperately to confront and affirm the totality of experience.

This is not to say that Nietzsche would have us discard our symbol systems, dispensing with fictions and rationalizations. He urged the rejection merely of those which demonstrably fail to promote our resolve to live and present ourselves. He would have us affirm each moment not for the sake of some supernatural purpose or some objective morality, but for our own sake. There is no alternative: "He who no longer finds what is great in God will find it nowhere — he must either deny or create it," Nietzsche wrote in *Zarathustra*.

Exemplifying rather than defending the need to be creative, Nietzsche's work constitutes an uncompromising, disciplined affirmation of man's autonomy in a world in which nothing can be taken for granted — not the record of history, not the predictions of positivist science, not the dictates of those in power, not the imperatives of Christian dogma, not the demands of an abstract rationality, not the pieties of his or any other day. Although Nietzsche subverted all these, he was no mere annihilator. The very existence of his work testifies to a positive morality — that of *publicizing annihilation as an ongoing act.* Disconfirming and unmasking all beliefs, he nonetheless confirmed that temper which keeps human enterprises (including that of empirical science) in motion: the combination of attachment and detachment necessary to engage in an interminable process for falsifying old beliefs by advancing new ones. Enjoining men to act, to play all the roles they can, he implied that they should embrace whatever discipline enables them to comprehend a maximum range of experience — and to reject whatever hinders comprehension. Affirm everything, he intoned, and redeem whatever deadly powers hinder affirmation by affirming those as well.

In the final analysis, the body of Nietzsche's writing constitutes a vindication of procedures which free men from needless, self-destructive clutter, from repressive institutions and beliefs, from whatever prevents them from affirming as much of themselves as they dare expose to public view. He assailed all impediments to self-expression (including grammar) — save those which experience shows to intensify, refine, and extend man's will to express himself. He made clear that the highest good is public freedom, the establishment of open spaces in which men who have tired of aiming at ready-made targets will be free to meet so as to design their own and test their skills. His perspective constitutes an appreciation of men not as victims or servants who passively bear witness to the truth but as artists who arrogantly presume to construct it, who make up whatever truths (or falsehoods) serve their need to acknowledge one another as beings forever in process of expressing themselves.

Celebrating man in action, Nietzsche took note of the variety of masks and uniforms he wears, his manifold styles and forms, his roles and performances, his covers and lies — all adopted and useful not because they reveal truth but because they amplify his existence:

> In man, the art of simulation reaches its peak: here deception, flattery, lying and cheating, talking behind the back, posing, living in borrowed splendor, being masked, the disguise of convention, acting a role before others and before oneself . . . is so much the rule and the law that almost nothing is more incomprehensible than how an honest and pure urge for truth could make its appearance among men.

The manifold expressions of this very "urge for truth" Nietzsche saw as appearances concealing the more basic urge for recognition. And as for truth per se: "nature threw away the key." Truth is but "a mobile army of metaphors, metonyms, and anthropomorphisms—in short, a sum of human relations, which have been enhanced, transposed, and embellished poetically and rhetorically, and which after long use seem firm, canonical, and obligatory to a people: truths are illusions about which one has forgotten that this is what they are."[4]

Nietzsche's premises turned out to be identical to those which led Marx to argue that so-called truths—the latest of which was the moral philosophy of the bourgeoisie—are but elite-serving ideologies and that, if the proletariat is to determine its own fate, all belief *systems* would have to be shown up for what they were—ideological weapons of the class in power for maintaining itself. Georges Sorel displayed an even greater appreciation for the uses of falsehoods: the masses, he insisted, could in fact never be mobilized without a leadership ready to use illusions, ideologies, or myths. There was no avoiding deceptions, no escape from having men appear in one or another disguise *and acting as if the masks were real.*

Yet Sorel felt it did remain possible to discriminate among competing deceptions, at least not to permit any specific one to become entrenched. One might seek to minimize the hold abstractions have on men, rely on Nietzsche and the voluntaristic elements of Marx, and fully use the inspirational power of myths to create a state in which man exists without any indubitable truth, whether certified by some party, class, race, or group of professionals.

Hannah Arendt, writing after the Second World War, elucidated what such an existence would involve. Having experienced and delineated twentieth-century totalitarianism in its fullest conceivable form, having idealized it, she faced the collapse of all conventional foundations and, like Nietzsche, sought to affirm what could no longer be denied:

> Whether we like it or not, we have long ceased to live in a world in which the faith in the Judeo-Christian myth of creation is secure enough to constitute a basis and source of authority for actual laws . . .

61

Our new difficulty is that we start from a fundamental distrust of everything merely given, a distrust of all laws and prescriptions, moral or social, that are deduced from a given comprehensive universal whole. This difficulty involves the sources of authority of law and questions the ultimate goals of political organizations and communities; it forces us not only to find and devise new laws, but to find and devise their very measure, the yardstick of good and evil, the principle of their source. For man, in the sense of the nature of man, is no longer the measure, despite what the new humanists would have us believe. Politically, this means that before drawing up the constitution of a new body politic, we shall have to create—not merely discover—a new foundation for human community as such.

In historical terms this would mean not the end of history, but its first consciously planned beginning.[5]

Without making the point explicit, Arendt defined the ground on which man is now entitled to proceed. It turned out to be what she called political space, that infinitely variable public arena Aristotle had defined as appropriate for political action. Quoting Aristotle, Arendt tellingly identified it as

the space of appearance in the widest sense of the word, the space where I appear to others as others appear to me, where men exist not merely like other living or inanimate things but make their appearance explicitly ... To be deprived of it means to be deprived of reality, which, humanly and politically speaking, is the same as appearance. To men the reality of the world is guaranteed by the presence of others, by its appearing to all; "for what appears to all, this we call Being," and whatever lacks this appearance comes and passes away like a dream, intimately and exclusively our own but without reality.[6]

Man's distinctive need can be understood as no less and emphatically no more than the use of his capacity to remain in the process of becoming, to gain recognition by making witnessed and comprehended appearances, thereby emerging as significant to others.

American pragmatic philosophy had made much the same point but without troubling to call attention to its political character. That the space in which men act so as to expand their awareness has all the attributes of political space was in fact so axiomatic to William James, John Dewey, and George Herbert Mead that they never explicitly defined it as such. John Dewey and Arthur Bentley, collaborating to write *Knowing and the Known,* simply gave no thought to politics when they defined the term "environment":

> *"Environment" is not something around and about human activities in an external sense; it is their* medium, *or* milieu, *in the sense in which a* medium *is* intermediate *in the execution or carrying* out *of human activities, as well as being the channel* through *which they move and the vehicle* by *which they go on. Narrowing of the medium is the direct source of all unnecessary impoverishment in human living; the only sense in which "social" is an honorific term is that in which the medium in which human living goes on is one by which human life is enriched.*[7]

To act on this definition is to keep enlarging the sphere of social action until resistance is met. It is to demote such nouns as cause, decision, design, knowledge, and value, converting these into verbs: causing, deciding, designating, knowing, and valuing.[8] Dewey and Bentley found support for their process orientation in Clerk Maxwell's account of the way physical science moved from "a conception of natural phenomena as the result of forces acting between one body and another" toward a new conception — one "in which the energy of a material system is conceived as determined by the configuration and motion of that system, and in which the ideas of configuration, motion, and force are generalized to the utmost extent warranted by their physical definitions."[9]

In America, Maxwell's key terms — "configuration, motion, and force" — were easy to universalize. They seemed to have general applicability, neither social critics nor philosophers recognizing a private sector to which such terms might not apply. Yet even while pragmatists talked as if politics actually permeated America, they unwittingly disclosed that this was less than the truth, that they were in fact idealizing, moving ahead of known experience, establishing a point of view. They created a new sensibility, an awareness of the *political* character of so-called private acts. In their perspective, all men who play a part in life's games — even a seemingly private part — began to emerge as actors using public time in public space. Action became public by definition, was *made* public by virtue of Bentley's and Dewey's verbal act.

Mead's approach was no different. Looking at the performances of scientists and historians, he quite simply saw them as political beings — though he, too, did not feel impelled to speak of politics. He contended that human actors were best known in an evolutionary process, their continuous encounters with troublesome obstacles inducing them not only to divide their labor and play specialized roles but also to coordinate their various activities by visualizing them from the standpoint of others, by engaging in acts Mead did not bother to call political. He saw men performing in relation to abstract forms which they consciously formulated. And consciousness, Mead held, was carried to its highest point by science defined as a problem-solving enterprise, defined as man's deliberate effort to keep enlarging the world of meaningful experience by a trial-and-error method. Thus Mead could conclude that the scientific method was but the evolutionary process grown self-conscious. Men evolved and gained in consciousness insofar as they were recurrently interrupted by obstacles they identified as problems. The scientific method, accordingly, was most basically a form of conduct, a self-imposed discipline. As such, it compelled men to form concepts and design laws with which to orient and compose and please themselves. It compelled the elimination of concepts and laws which can be shown not to suit men. Even such notions as time and space, categories in which science had once made the world appear to us in order to enable us to humanize it, are not simply to be accepted as suitable, as miraculously given prior to experience (in this, Mead accepted Hegel and amended Kant).

Instead, time and space are created in the very process of experience, as part of our effort to overcome obstacles—and, as Mead said, we ourselves are responsible for them.[10] Depending on our variable interests, categories are conceived, refined, and *made* true by methods we find useful to cope with our problems, to satisfy our needs, to care for ourselves.

This evolutionary, genetic approach to concept formation in the sciences could be seen as no less applicable to the design of interpretative schemes in the discipline of history.[11] In fact, all communication issues in symbolic forms—finally, as Dewey was to note in detail, in what we call works of art. The creative process in the physical sciences, the social sciences, or the arts—collectively, the humanities—will again and again come to some culmination. To catch our breath, to act, we need to arrest events, fix the flux of life, just as we use words which signify shared perceptions to *hold* reality and *frame* experience. Art, as Dewey defined it, is a crystallized manifestation of man's intentions, intentions which, when stabilized, constitute a publicly meaningful reality. Works of art make experience known: they momentarily establish and publicize "purposes that outrun evidence." Stating unrealized ends, they express the meaning of human action and provide the basis for continuing it. For Dewey, therefore, cognition itself was an activity, that is, goal-oriented action. Unless we aim, unless we seek to make a point, he maintained, there can be no cognition. Frozen theory and fluid life, abstract reason and concrete will, are thus fused; public knowledge is the outcome—always renewable—of the integrated movement of conscious activity, of deliberate experimentation, of controlled rage. It is the wholly natural consequence of man's protean impulse to project and present himself—and to know all the while that attempting less diminishes him. Thus knowing and valuing, as William James wrote, become one and the same, a fused form of action:

> *I, for my part, cannot escape the consideration, forced upon me at every turn, that the knower is not simply a mirror floating with no foot-hold anythere, and passively reflecting an order that he comes upon and finds simply existing. The knower is an actor, and coefficient of the*

truth which he helps to create. Mental interests, hypotheses, postulates, so far as they are bases for human action—action which to a great extent transforms the world—help to make the truth which they declare.[12]

The view of man's truth-making role which had found expression in American pragmatic philosophizing was wholly shared by the literature of European existentialism. Departing from Hegel, this literature stressed that the ultimate source of theoretical systems (to which Marxists added tangible economic systems) is man's irreducible will to assert himself in the face of whatever forces threaten to degrade him. The perennial theme of existentialist writing is that the root of all forms of thought and action is our determination to confer meaning on experience by expressing it. We are burdened, it was affirmed, by nature and by others, by knowledge of the past and the future; we necessarily experience pain and troubles, and are ultimately extinguished. Seeking to defy necessity, we must rely on ourselves, for there is no authority for anyone's claim that some transcending purpose gives meaning to our existence. When honest with ourselves, we will accept a life without center or horizon, one within which no truth, god, finality, or meaning is vouchsafed for us. As we project ourselves, create options, and put our various resources to the test, we consequently cannot in good faith believe that we are limited by any set of static laws ostensibly derived from some objective realm of absolutes. We must acknowledge that we have but ourselves and that we can identify our limits not by conforming to some preexisting order of reality but rather by making our appearance in as many diverse ways as our capacities allow.

Meaningful experience, in sum, is ours to formulate and enlarge, reality ours to define. Defining situations as real (to paraphrase W. I. Thomas), we make them real for ourselves.[13] We act upon the world, and our acts—our symbol systems, our factual accounts, our social performances, our political institutions, our very personalities—emerge as works of art.

Knowledge through Empathy

If all our acts are works of art, how might they be most appropriately comprehended? What mode of cognition would make

66

them most fully accessible to us? In 1725, Giambattista Vico provided clues that were to become the background for a reformulated theory of knowledge—or better, for a new way of getting to know man's works. In his *New Science* he wrote that there was "a truth beyond all question: that the world of human society has certainly been made by men, and its principles are therefore to be found within the modifications of our own human mind."[14] This "truth beyond all question" could serve to reinforce not only Kant's view of man as disposed to construct his world through symbols but also Hobbes's basis for knowledge of human actions. Vico's argument is clear enough: we can know only what we are involved with, most directly what we make; purposefully acting so as to realize our ideals, we make our societies; hence it is possible to gain knowledge of human societies to the extent that we

> *The understanding of the human drama not only comes out of participation in the drama, but is participation in the drama—and, incidentally, playwriting, casting, and personnel production all together.*
>
> —John R. Seeley
> "The Americanization of the Unconscious"
>   (1967)

can understand human purposes. Insofar as institutions are expressions of man's purposes, intentions, wishes, actions, and motives, we can penetrate the facades of society and know their inner meaning. As we can know our own and one another's minds, we can know what our minds have expressed in history: cultural artifacts, civil laws, scientific operations, styles of life. In Isaiah Berlin's words, Vico formulated for the first time

> *the principle according to which man can understand himself because, and in the process, of understanding his past—because he is able to reconstruct imaginatively (in Aristotle's phrase) what he did and what he suffered,*

his hopes, wishes, fears, efforts, his acts, and his works,
both his own and those of his fellows. With their experi-
ences his own is interwoven, his own and his (and their)
ancestors', whose monuments, customs, laws, but, above
all, words, still speak to him; indeed, if they did not, and
if he did not understand them, he would not understand
his fellows' or his own symbols, he would not be able to
communicate or think or conceive purposes, to form so-
cieties or become fully human.

Vico identified a new way of knowing, maintaining that we can
gain knowledge by sympathetically entering into the mental life
of historical actors. As Berlin has pointed out, Vico not only applied the maxim that "one can fully know only what one has
made to such provinces as mathematics, mythology, symbolism,
language," Vico also "uncovered a sense of knowing which is
basic to all humane studies: the sense in which I know what it
is to be poor, to fight for a cause, to belong to a nation, to join or
abandon a church or a party, to feel nostalgia, terror, the omni-
presence of a god, to understand a gesture, a work of art, a joke,
a man's character, that one is transformed or lying to oneself."
We gain such knowledge by acts of empathic insight, by imaginatively intuiting the essential, typical quality of whatever we confront, by seeking to know not *that* something is so and so, or *how*
something came about but rather what, given its appearance,
something must be when seen, as it were, from the inside. Berlin's elaboration helps to make the point:

> *This is the sort of knowing which participants in an ac-*
> *tivity claim to possess as against mere observers: the*
> *knowledge of the actors, as against that of the audience,*
> *of the "inside" story as opposed to that obtained from*
> *some "outside" vantage point; knowledge by "direct*
> *acquaintance" with my "inner" states or by sympathetic*
> *insight into those of others, which may be obtained by a*
> *high degree of imaginative power; the knowledge that is*
> *involved when a work of the imagination or of social*
> *diagnosis or a work of criticism or scholarship or history*
> *is described not as correct or incorrect, skillful or inept,*

a success or a failure, but as profound or shallow, realistic or unrealistic, perceptive or stupid, alive or dead . . .

The past can be seen through the eyes—the categories and ways of thinking, feeling, imagining—of at any rate possible inhabitants of possible worlds, of associations of men brought to life by what, for want of a better phrase, we call imaginative insight. There must exist a capacity for conceiving (or at least a claim to be able to conceive) what "it must have been like" to think, feel, act, in Homeric Greece, in the Rome of the Twelve Tables, in Phoenician colonies given to human sacrifice, or in cultures less remote or exotic, but still requiring suspension of the most deep-lying assumptions of the inquirer's own civilization. It cannot be otherwise if one is to begin to achieve any understanding of the "inner" structure of something outside one's immediate range of vision.[15]

The aspects of life which lie outside our immediate range of vision are not of course only some historical past—one we can reconstruct by supplying ourselves with a history of consciousness—but also the unseen present. That is, we can gain understanding of the unseen aspects of our contemporaries, of presently ignored, marginal, repressed interests. Their meaning—their very presence—will become known when we suspend the notion that knowledge must be based on overt behavior registered by the senses, that, as detached nonpartisans, we can only take man's measure from the outside.

To gain knowledge of men ignored by conventional history or conventional sociology, we must enter into the lives of others, locating ourselves in their cultures—their villages, housing projects, political parties, educational or religious institutions. Following Vico, Johann Gottfried von Herder was to provide a basis for precisely such participatory ventures. He rejected the belief that some enduring abstract rationality guided the whole of mankind: to understand men we must attend to cultural variation, to the infinite number of ways men express themselves, each culture possessing its own consciousness, own dynamic, own structure, own validity. Only knowledge of the specific and

69

unique context of human action can yield knowledge of its meaning. No abstractions transcending the unique can ultimately hold; no generalization can be regarded as finally valid—for all eliminate the felt diversity of experience. Theories, explanations, analogies, metaphors, words—these have to be brought down to earth, into touch with men and women existing in specific settings.

The practical problem, of course, is first how to escape the metaphysical mists of philosophy and the abstractions of positivistic science, next how to identify and turn directly to the phenomena, and then how to express and communicate one's new experience. One has to delete (Edmund Husserl was to speak of "bracketing") the preconceptions about other cultures which one's own culture has implanted, risking a deflation of given values, accepting moral relativism. This does not mean, as George Devereux has stressed, that others can be encountered without accepting subjectively or ethnocentrically established ways of classifying them.[16] To become aware of others, some footing must be postulated, and a familiar footing is least likely to make us lose our balance. Without some secure point of departure—some localized source for judgment—we do not have the leverage for moving ahead, for perceiving and expressing new experiences. Having identified our specific self in a social context, we can discern and drop needless defenses, moving (like Melville's Ishmael) as close to the phenomena as possible, joining up with them— except for one decisive difference between them and us, namely, our own conscious resolve to outlive them and to give the fullest possible expression to our experience.

Unless we communicate, unless we symbolize our experience, we succumb to the spell of the particular and drown in experience. Failing to express ourselves, we become one-dimensional, dead to alternatives, exclusively committed to our latest involvement. But if we continue to signal, to keep a log, or to write letters out into the world, we can keep connecting with others. And as others hear and know us, the balance of their interests is enlarged as well. Our interests—our very lives—thus expand not as we accumulate unfalsified, potentially usable propositions in some storehouse but rather as we are engaged in the very process of communicating our understanding of situations.

70

Since experience is appropriated only insofar as it is understood, gains in experience and gains in knowledge are inextricably one.

That efforts to expand one's experience should be seen as acts to expand one's understanding—as acts of imaginative empathy—was argued during the first quarter of the twentieth century by a generation of German writers concerned with the philosophy of the social sciences.[17] Empathic acts, they argued somewhat laboriously, serve to give resonance and integrity to human efforts and thereby make them accessible to wider publics. As we deliberately reexperience in our own consciousness the experiences which gave rise to the acts of others—as we recognize compassion in the sound of a command, gratitude in the movement of a hand, hatred in the maintenance of a smile—we see a new dimension. Our new vision imposes order on feelings which eluded us before and which our new involvements aroused in us. We relate behavior (a smile) to the purpose (hatred) that had given it significance. We recognize men as actors. And watching ourselves articulating our new experiences, we secure knowledge of the acts of others, defining their struggle to contain their wayward pains and pleasures, to express themselves. We thus perceive ourselves and others enacting human order, creating forms, structures, roles, styles, frameworks, categories. We recognize our welter of institutions—especially the institution of language—as human enactments deliberately brought into being. We see ourselves in relation to the rules, rituals, languages, and procedures necessary for coping with our troubles, for enduring in a world which fails to disclose its inner meaning.

When unaware of these implicit rules—the unspoken protocol which gives coherence to the seemingly incoherent act of a politician, a surgeon, a priest, a warrior, a slave—we see only what meets the eye (or the measuring instruments which refine our vision). The basic point made by sociologists from Max Weber to Alfred Schutz is that unless we publicly acknowledge the tacit dimensions of overt behavior—the images in relation to which men manage to conduct themselves—our knowledge of society will remain needlessly partial. Unless our cognitive activity gives credence to the standards or rules men intend to approximate in practice, we remain ignorant of the man-made, distinctively political aspects of human existence.

Cognitive activity has the effect of making unfamiliar, invisible forms of life familiar and visible. Raising them to the level of consciousness, amplifying them, it makes them available and usable. Thus Max Weber disclosed the rational coherence of seemingly irrational impulses in his *Protestant Ethic and the Spirit of Capitalism*, while Erving Goffman disclosed the good sense of procedures which serve confidence men to "cool off the mark," which serve those in power to quiet down those marked for defeat in the games of life. When ostensibly irrational forms of action are brought out into open political space, when the sociologist or novelist *or whoever* succeeds in expressing them, one universe of symbols is translated into another. When successful, such translations yield knowledge of the specific way in which the original exists: they restate the distinctive forms of human acts, whether these acts are literary productions, mathematical exercises, military strategies, parliamentary maneuvers, or, most comprehensively, the decisions made to maintain political communities. A successful translation will provide understanding of each of these activities as one among various possible ones — but in any case as an expression of man's need to communicate, to give a communicable *form* to experience. It was Weber especially who made evident that students of society cannot presume to know what is meant by such acts as a legislative bill, a presidential inaugural, a state dinner, a ghetto riot, or a city plan if these are seen as mere functions of an autonomous, self-maintaining system, as mere byproducts or effects of some preestablished reality. To know their antecedent causes is not to know what they signify. No causal explanation can make the significance of our acts intelligible. They must be seen as wholes, as autonomous manifestations of human endeavor. By elaborating their contexts and explicating their implications, we give them integrity. By imputing significance to human acts, by referring them to more than they *are* — to more than the powerful claim them to *be* — we connect action with previously unseen and unforeseen phenomena — with motives, intentions, purposes.

The visible and the invisible, actuality and potentiality, thereby become integral components of a field, a totality to be understood as such. *What can thus be understood is not merely an aggregation of present data — the addition or multiplication of distinct features or events — but the structure of the whole, its essential form.* Such understanding comes about by acts of focus-

> As any art form — for that, finally, is what we are dealing with — the cockfight renders ordinary, everyday experience comprehensible by presenting it in terms of acts and objects which have had their practical consequences removed and been reduced (or, if you prefer, raised) to the level of sheer appearances, where their meaning can be more powerfully articulated and more exactly perceived. The cockfight is "really real" only to the cocks — it does not kill anyone, castrate anyone, reduce anyone to animal status, alter the hierarchical relations among people, nor refashion the hierarchy; it does not even redistribute income in any significant way. What it does is what, for other peoples with other temperaments and other conventions, Lear and Crime and Punishment do; it catches up these themes — death, masculinity, rage, pride, loss, beneficence, chance — and, ordering them into an encompassing structure, presents them in such a way as to throw into relief a particular view of their essential nature. It puts a construction on them, makes them, to those historically positioned to appreciate the construction, meaningful — visible, tangible, graspable — "real," in an ideational sense. An image, fiction, a model, a metaphor, the cockfight is a means of expression; its function is neither to assuage social passions nor to heighten them (though, in its play-with-fire way, it does a bit of both), but, in a medium of feathers, blood, crowds, and money, to display them.
>
> —Clifford Geertz
> "The Balinese Cockfight" (1972)

ing. Deliberately distancing ourselves to integrate and comprehend progressively more of experience, we can, as in a flash, *see* it. We may then claim to have acted so as to get an idea of it, an

73

idea which the facts themselves have no power to disclose — facts never being striking or revealing until our ideas succeed in making them striking or revealing.

As our vision establishes increasingly comprehensive contexts for specific experiences, we *make* experiences more comprehensible. Breaking open and seeing through a seemingly closed reality, disregarding the prevailing order of so-called facts, we renew old meanings or bring new ones into our presence. We find ourselves *playing* God, *acting* on the presumptuous notion that we ourselves can bring order out of chaos.

To be sure, we may be mistaken in our assumption that men or societies are more than meets the eye. Surely not all men are actors maintaining their balance. Not all forms of behavior signify the presence of an invisible dimension. Nor are all men motivated to make an appearance and communicate. Turbulence within a community or the outcry of a victim may equally well be convulsive, an involuntary, uncontrolled *re*action. Who would deny that some individuals (or groups) suffer from hysteria, paralysis, or amnesia, that some lives are nothing but accidents, that some men exist in catatonic or frenzied states in which they do nothing by choice? Surely, men do not always play games. Hence we exaggerate if we claim (with Shakespeare's Jacques) that all the world's a stage, or (with Erving Goffman) that all life is drama, or (with R. S. Peters) that all individuals are chess players writ large. But such exaggerations are no different from (and as true as) the exaggerations embodied in all ideals. They are operative lies, like myths, designed to arouse, to release adrenalin, to give nerve and energy to tired and enervated men.[18] If life is not a play, it may yet become one by our giving recognition and status to apparent abnormalities of conduct, by our establishing contextual fields of operation, that is, by our defining the essential ground for insurgent behavior, apathy, schizophrenia, or fanaticism.

If our interest lies in enlarging arenas in which men live by choice, in which they live deliberately, we must doubt the dismal conclusion to which past experience has driven us, the confirmed knowledge that men recurrently behave as brutes. We must give others the benefit of our doubt. Distrusting well-known experience, we must be willing to suspect there is always more to it than we permit ourselves to know, conceding that even when assassins stand up, they do so to be counted. The perception of others as persons in charge of themselves may in fact turn out to be a self-fulfilling act: communicating our perception to men who are nearly out of control, we build their self-esteem and enable them to escape their brute-like condition.

Of course we may still have sufficient reason to doubt that someone else's act was expressive ("given the pressures on him, what else could he do but stand up and be counted?"). To protect ourselves against assaults by men out of control (and to protect them against themselves), we rightly rely on such knowledge as we happen to have. Yet the whole thrust of the theorizing of pragmatists, existentialists, and phenomenologists is such as to warn us not to use all our resources for protecting ourselves against others: we need others to be ourselves.

When we suspend disbelief and use what power we have to ascribe human qualities to others, we serve ourselves even if it should turn out that we failed to serve them. Not only are we then induced to recall impulses of our own, discovering capacities for action we had forgotten or repressed. We also learn to define experiences we have obviously not had but may still be capable of having. Moreover, we will have provided ourselves with new factual details, new colors, textures, and tones, new environments in which to act. These are not negligible consequences of doubting the findings of the social sciences. When we are denied access to new public spaces—to repressed parts of ourselves— because of the solid knowledge given by the prevailing political science, we have reason for welcoming a persuasion which makes men more nervous, civilization more precarious, and human life more protean.

V

Inconclusiveness as Ideal

It assuredly is possible to collect diverse works focusing on human nature to sift out a view of man as nothing but creator of facts, as wholly determined to impose his own order on an inherently meaningless universe. Yet no such view is simply to be found. Furthermore, once sifted out, it still must be made presentable. Whoever presumes to present it, as I have tried, must make concessions, adjusting his vision to the sensibilities of his patrons, his readers, even his alter ego. Thus I have misleadingly —though usefully—suggested that the uncomplicated catch-phrases of mere summaries actually express past commitments to man as political actor. To make philosophers as diverse, for example, as Hobbes and Arendt appear as if they had been contributors to a shared position is to engage in the construction of a past—all the more obviously and irritatingly so when some of the very writers I have called to testify explicitly decline to take *any* position. Yet I have still wished to use them—or at least wished to use what for my purposes is best in them.

No wonder, then, that I have become inventive, established continuities, and made connections: I have discerned (or tendentiously created) support for my own idealized abstraction. To serve my present purpose, I have set things up so as to make it appear that disparate thinkers converge. I have quoted out of context, relying on the pretense that this is avoidable. Using such dramatic stratagems as raising questions, providing partial answers, raising further questions, and maintaining suspense, I have sought to grant a patent, so to speak, to a deliberately postulated ideal—in this case to a model consciously designed to free men to develop the political potentialities inherent in their existence.

The Precarious Present

To depict men as naturally disposed to make every situation in which they find themselves governable by their joint action is to emphasize the autonomy of their will. It is to show men perennially resolving to transform the chaos they confront into some imagined order. In a model of man without given qualities— man as will incarnate—artistic and scientific acts are seen as generated by the tension between their oppressive, nonpolitical experiences and the conviction—given status by our imagination— that things might be otherwise, that there are still unconfirmed experiences, unrealized realities. Men confront the world and ask, first in wonder but ultimately with exasperated resentment, "Could *this* be?" And they proceed to project new possibilities, designing futures which seem to be precluded by the prevailing organization of society. They imagine unfamiliar, easily cursed dimensions of themselves. Their imagination empowers them to humanize these unfamiliar aspects of their lives, to play roles they had not played before. They seek to test and act on whatever has fallen (or emerged) within the range of their experience. When they can make themselves assume that the meaning of whatever they know to be present must have been imposed by someone with power to designate and signify, to establish good and evil, they can approach both the past and the future—whatever is *now* alleged to be known—as still in process. They become confident that their world can be envisaged and acted upon anew, that it can be experienced differently. And by forming and reforming their experiences, by communicating them, they will have made them public. The incredible happens: their world becomes political insofar as they share their ideas, metaphors, concepts, and theories with others. They literally enact their ideas, the limit of their action set only by the economic and emotional resources for testing what is ostensibly real and necessary, ostensibly nonpolitical. Their designs—and these include individuals who, by design, become public figures, persons, actors—

78

are therefore always subject to re-view and re-vision, subject to change.

Far from making man a mindless exploiter of his environment, the model I am here sketching reveals him as taking care of himself and others, infinitely mindful of his own need to act so as to keep his world and himself continuously open to human use. Disposed to *remain* in control, he is not free to demean himself or despoil his world; the forms he imposes save and augment life so that his political impulse will be continuously served. Being reflective, he takes steps likely to enhance his capacity for creating roles, acting out alternatives, and making appearances. Though he may act as if he did feel morally responsible to some transcendent standard, I would see him as merely obeying his own constitution, designing himself and building institutions which enable him progressively to enlarge the sphere of politics — that is, of life deliberately lived.

This model specifies that for political life, no present structure — no order of facts — can be deemed irrevocably necessary. Conversely, whatever is shown by experimental action to be unchangeable and unavoidable must be treated as nonpolitical, or at least as not yet political. When consciously made, this distinction between freedom (men acting in the sphere defined as political) and necessity (men helplessly reacting to laws not of their own making, to forces they do not control) has the effect of organizing activities: it serves to make attempts to minimize necessity and maximize freedom more coherent and effective.

This does not mean that necessity might ultimately be surmounted by some apocalyptic project. Man's very nature, as Karl Marx observed, limits his freedom:

> *Just as the savage must wrestle with Nature to satisfy his wants, to maintain and to reproduce his life, so must civilized man, and he must do so in all social formations and under all possible modes of production. With his development this realm of physical necessity expands, as do his wants; but at the same time the forces which satisfy these wants also increase. In this field, freedom can only consist in that socialized man, the associated producers, rationally regulate their metabolic inter-*

79

change with nature, bringing it under their control instead
of being ruled by it as by blind forces, and achieve this
with the least expenditure of energy and under conditions
most favourable to and worthy of their human nature.
But it always will remain a realm of necessity. *Beyond it*
begins the development of human energy which is con-
sidered an end in itself, the true empire of freedom, which,
however, can blossom forth only with the realm of neces-
sity as its basis.[1]

To accept Marx's distinction is at once to avoid sentimental
utopianism—the notion that we might crash into some heaven of
pure creativity—and to fire the imagination by raising the possibility that we may develop "the true empire of freedom."

Impelled to keep extending the sphere of politics, we can
adopt the standard succinctly formulated by William James:
"That act is the best act which makes for the best whole, the best
whole being that which prevails at least cost, in which the van-
quished goods are least completely annulled,"[2] This "best whole"
may be seen as that inclusive state which Aristotle identified as
man's most comprehensive good—an order which aims at integrating partial goods, fosters individual growth by providing the
ground for encounters with others, and promotes self-esteem by
enabling individuals to discern and govern their conflicting
interests.

Political institutions, in this model, elicit and order the
infinite variety of possible human concerns; they succeed in
bringing the various schemes of individuals out into the open and
into a state of balance. They constrain and temper special interests
by making each of their advocates conscious of the partisan character of their claims. Inducing men to see themselves as others
see them, they facilitate participation, thereby heightening individual consciousness and expanding the range of human sympathy. They compel men to recognize the needs of others and to
deny themselves the security of final victory. When well designed, such institutions will lead men to desire nothing more
final than a state of permanently unresolved conflict.

The Political Animal

In the terms of this model, the politically mature individual seeks to maintain a state of conflict by checking and balancing his various concerns so that none can get the best of him, so that none can become exclusively valid. He extends his interests by embracing those of others, including those which deprive him of his present comforts. He realizes that as long as he lives he is less than "mature," for he is not only concerned with being "balanced" and "maintaining political stability" but also with incorporating additional interests, forever enlarging the existing balance. He thus expresses in concentrated form the ideal of every political order, of all human enterprises. Karl Deutsch's discussion of growth makes explicit what is entailed:

> *Growth should mean not merely the highest degree of unity and self-determination within the existing limits of a system . . . nor should growth mean a mere enlargement of the system with no change in its characteristics of performance . . . Rather, growth also should mean an application of learning capacity toward an increase in openness, that is, an increase in the range, diversity, and effectiveness of an organization's channels of intake of information from the outside world . . . Still further, growth should mean an increase in an organization's ability to make effective responses to its environment and to change this environment in accordance with its need . . . And, finally, growth should mean an increase in the range and diversity of goals the organization is able to follow, including the power to change goals and to add new ones.*[3]

In the light of this formulation, it should be clear, men must be defined as preeminently innovating beings who favor not any specific objective but rather whatever policies are apt to *keep* them innovating without causing them to lose their balance in the process. They mediate their private passions within a public arena, within structures encouraging them to recognize one another and communicate. Such structures, Aristotle was the first to argue, are wholly natural to men. Their creation and maintenance is the only interest men have in common. When men are not enslaved by nature or by one another, they can acknowledge no higher good, no other public interest.

This ideal conception of political life and the public interest cannot, of course, be simply derived from what we know to be experience. The obstinate fact is that most men most of the time do *not* govern themselves. Again and again, men are out of control, compulsively driven, compelled by their pains to conform to forces outside themselves. Over vast stretches of the globe and of history, men have been without the freedom even to become aware of their paralyses and their spasms, of their apathy, frenzy, and trembling. In less extreme terms, men have generally not been free to play roles but constrained to play them, being cast or outcast, being fitted into social systems in which they were assigned parts. Or they have been permitted to keep trying on different masks and uniforms until they could finally discover what they were expected to wear, what roles they might *safely* take. But if their lives are frequently not so much lived as being lived, this may be due not to the obstinate, fixed nature of man but to changeable conditions. Whether or not men are able to control these conditions, the fact is that the mass of men have hardly had the opportunity to be political.

This lack of opportunity is rarely called to their attention. Impressed by democracy as a threat to stability, the beneficiaries of prevailing orders are not likely to place their privileges in jeopardy. It is in any case understandable why social scientists should have painstakingly taken note of the nonpolitical, dependent condition of man and treated it as necessary and rational, characterizing alternatives as unrealistic. Sensitive to the loosening of man's economic dependency and social bonds, wanting order, social scientists have not minded pointing out that man is essentially unfree, that he is a *biological* being (forced to respond to genetic, neurological, and territorial imperatives), an *economic* being (forced to provide for his subsistence), or a *social* being (forced to play roles not of his making)—but in any case not a *political* being.

To formulate a conception of political man, political sci-

82

entists therefore cannot merely orient themselves by what is demonstrably "natural" or "real," by the prevailing nonpolitical forces which have found articulate representatives among social scientists. Political scientists cannot subscribe to the norm which makes present experience the source of valid scientific generalizations, which induces them to believe that, to be "realistic," their generalizations must be derived from "the facts." Instead, they must test the obstinacy of the alleged facts, learn (by doing) whether the facts might be otherwise, whether imaginative acts might not deprive the facts of their hold on society. This entails efforts to locate and control the stimuli to which men helplessly respond, efforts to come to terms with the constraints which a positivistic social science rightly shows to be manifestly present at the center of our lives.

If the altogether "realistic" accounts of a positivistic science of man only show how, *as a rule*, men behave, if they are not designed to yield an unrealized model of political man, political scientists should find it useful to turn to barely recorded, ill-articulated, marginal intimations of human possibilities—not to the rules, but to the exceptions which can become rules when men have power to make them such. Political scientists can seek to delineate a model of political man by turning away from portraits of conventional heroes and looking for life styles which have been variously celebrated, whether in the ancient posture of Diogenes, in the modern stance of Dostoevsky's underground man, in contemporary fiction and films prefigured in *Don Quixote,* in the educational theory of Rousseau, or in the ideal of psychological health most recently defined by such social psychologists as Gordon Allport.[4]

While I can discern a coherent image of human nature in these various formulations, I find it hard to describe this image in language that will not reduce man to some specific bundle of immutable elements. The problem for me, for political scientists, for everyone is to treat biopsychological systems—the individual person as well as the body politic—as multifaceted and open-ended. They must be treated as if they *are* nothing, as if they amounted to nothing more than projects designed to make men appear in action. To understand political aspects of life, to see them as open to unexpressed and unanticipated possibilities, the perceptions of political scientists must be deliberately framed in ambiguous terms, in a playful, suspenseful, question-begging idiom. Just as an unambiguous, denotative, *serious* language refers to what men *are*, drawing verbal boundaries around settled or pacified areas within which men are indeed inactive, a consist-

> *I can deeply sympathize with anyone who objects to being tossed into such a floating cosmology. Much as I have stressed its substantiality, I can hardly expect everyone to feel it. The firm land of "matter" or even of "sense" or "self" is pleasanter, if only it stands firm. To anyone whose tasks can be performed on such ground, I have not the slightest thought of bringing disturbance. But for many of us tasks are pressing, in the course of which our finest spots of conventional departure themselves dissolve in function. When they have so dissolved, there is no hope of finding refuge in some chance island of "fact" which may appear. The continents go, and the islands.*
>
> —Arthur F. Bentley
> "Behavior Knowledge Fact" (1935)

ently equivocal language can keep pointing to indeterminate potentialities, to men and societies in process, intent on nothing more than acting.

What this perspective acknowledges as characteristic of societies in action is therefore not some fixed set of traits or objective properties but the continuous resolve of men to display themselves, to remain in motion by creating time and space beyond biopsychological necessity, to design progressively more intriguing masks and games for themselves. Men are seen as doing so not because any of this is *good* for something but because it enables them to make more parts of themselves visible and respectable. This perspective, moreover, makes room for multidimensional man, treating the body (man's physiochemical, bioecological nature) and the mind (his self-generated intentions) as fused when man acts to create, manage, and ultimately play with what we nicely call the facts of life.

The very ambiguity of their languages reveals how men resolve to defy necessity and assert as much of themselves as they dare. It opens closed doors with symbolic acts, with performances designed to master unfamiliar, ungoverned spaces. Using their imaginative faculties, men order wayward experiences, revealing a desire to cope with a progressively richer repertoire of roles. Given the opportunity, they seek to become more assertive and accomplished as well as more spectacular, dramatic, winning, and attractive—ever seeking to attract others by the scenes they steal or make, the roles they create, the alternative selves they present. Their preeminent concern is with presenting ourselves—gaining public recognition by making witnessed and comprehended appearances. Precisely this *and emphatically no more* is all that can be definitively affirmed by political science about the "nature" of man as a political being.

The Pragmatic Validation of Needs

Yet to free the individual to express himself in action is inevitably to raise the question of how far he should be free to go. How much self-expression—we should like someone to certify —is justified? How much is needed?

To these questions, however, there can be no set answer. "Ultimately," Amitai Etzioni has said, "there is no way for a societal structure to discover the members' needs and adapt to them without the participation of the members in shaping and reshaping the structure."[5] Unless we engage in common action, knowledge is denied us. What is more, participatory action is an epistemological imperative not only for the participants but also for the person who would prefer to remain the detached observer. He, too, must interact if he wishes to disclose what is needed by men. To give credibility to his statements, to have others share his expressions, he, too, must participate. For man, there is no exit.

The point is not that, because we cannot claim to have valid knowledge without acting, we must first of all act and subsequently "recollect in tranquillity," persuasively generalizing

85

from prior experience. Rather, action and knowledge are inextricably one. To be in action, is to know oneself to be in action; it is to be aware of alternatives, to discover one's capacities and thereby learn *precisely* what one can successfully manage. As we dramatize our ability to bring new interests into a publicly meaningful relationship, we are validating a new reality. It follows that we can never claim to have absolute, unconditional knowledge of "real" human needs essential to men in some ultimate (or original) state of nature.

The only knowledge we can ever claim to have at any one moment is conditional. Rejecting the implication of sequence, we must yet express ourselves in the conventional *if-then* form of experimental science: *if* you succeed in removing constraints x, y, and z, *then* you will probably manage to play not only well-known parts A and B, but also part C. Put differently: were "reality" changed, men could master a greater variety of experiences in more intensive ways. Their needs would then be more extensively and intensively satisfied.

Clearly, there is no alternative to testing, to participating in efforts to violate whatever is alleged to be reality, whatever equilibrium positivists certify to be real. Placing our bets, we will in each instant either have lost our wager or else compelled reality to yield, learning in the very process of acting that, to the extent that we succeed in pushing back the coercive forces of the wilderness or of society, we have gained in manageable experience, in meaningful political life. Winning means learning that we had not quite needed the prevailing discipline, the prevailing degree of postponed gratification—that we did not have to curse as much in life and in ourselves as we thought. And because we made our wager deliberately, we will not merely *feel* that there had been excessive constraints: we will *know*, and will be able to communicate our knowledge. Having felt we needed to live more amply, we will have learned in practice (if we survived) that we could. The facts will be on our side.

What we need—not necessarily what we want—can never be finally discovered: it is located nowhere to *be* discovered. Because our needs can only be realized in an experimental process which treats present systems of domination and necessity as if

86

they violated us, as if they frustrated us beyond our needs, it is best to remain silent about arrangements suitable for some future utopian community. There can be no post-experimental utopia,

> *The separation of the "deed" from the "doer,"*
> *of the events from someone who produces*
> *events, of the process from the something that*
> *is not process but enduring substance, thing,*
> *body, soul, etc.—the attempt to comprehend an*
> *event as a sort of shifting and place—changing*
> *on the part of a "being," of something constant:*
> *this ancient mythology established the belief*
> *in "cause and effect" after it had found a*
> *firm form in the functions of language and*
> *grammar.*
>
> —Friedrich Nietzsche
> "The Mechanistic Interpretation of the World"
>   (1885)

no final resting place—only the continuously communicated satisfaction of having reduced the insignificance of our existence. For man, in politics, utopia is here and now.

To be sure, a commitment to testing, to political life as an on-going, self-consciously conducted experiment, poses a welter of troublesome practical questions which no abstract theory can presume to answer. What should be done when it becomes evident that an experiment—like a revolution—is so intoxicating or exhausting that it makes participants frantic or listless, diminishing them even though they are in action? How should we respond when experimentation enrages opponents, making them so resentful of the extension of freedom that they proceed to stop us? Of course, we could appeal to a shared norm and urge all prospective participants to make only choices likely to make everyone's *continuous* action possible; we could exhort them *not* to provoke the strong or destroy the weak—*not* to violate whomever they

87

might yet need as irritants for promoting their own personal growth. We can remind them to be careful: every course of action closes some future options.

Yet in view of the practical complexities which confront us, it is hardly helpful to denounce self-destruction and praise self-enhancement. Forced to make specific choices while unable to see far ahead, responsible for the *totality* of ourselves (including future selves which include our present enemies), we are faced by the most practical problems of priorities and tactics, and we rightly demand predictions and solutions. We wish to know about our actual and prospective capacity for striking out for new territory without conventional comforts—be it the comfort of religion, ideology, mythology, ritual, consensus. Can we manage without faith in some sort of truth, in some given historical process, in some continuity? Are those firm traits we associate with "character" and "integrity" not required to enable us to take risks? Don't we need some fixed center, some consistent "identity"? Do we in fact have the capacity for overcoming the manifest present, for sustaining new forms of political consciousness, and for surviving within an enlarged political order? Can we pull ourselves together and act once we learn that nature gives no final answer, once we discover that its pervasive ambiguity leaves us free to choose the constraints which give significance to our lives? To what extent is it possible, in practice, to welcome a mode of action—a political science—which detaches us from prevailing social fortifications and empowers us to *be* something by remaining in process? If we cannot be wholly free from constraints, precisely how much repression (in the phrase of Herbert Marcuse) is necessary and how much is surplus?

The answers to these questions depend on currently available resources for learning about ourselves in practice. We are well served (not mobilized, not governed) by social scientists who are preoccupied by taking stock, who seek to note how much the existing system can bear and how much is overload, who estimate costs, consequences, and byproducts of alternative policies, and who specify what we *can* do by taking account of past failures. They can answer the question, as Max Weber posed it, of what "the realization of a devised end will cost in terms of the presumably inevitable destruction of other values."[6] The conclusions of positivistic forms of analysis—causal inquiries, comparative research, cost-benefit analyses—all have their uses. Admittedly, social scientists may respond to social and ideological pressure, abandon logic, and confuse their concepts with reality. Yet there is nothing in *logic* compelling causal analysis, cost-benefit accounts, or systems analysis to drive out other modes of inquiry and stabilize the status quo.[7] It would in any case be indefensible to reject positivistic efforts to inquire how our present enemies—our potential selves—behave under variable conditions.

Furthermore, when taking account of exceptional cases, positivistic studies may reveal that whoever in society makes demands, it is not "nature" but someone with the power to interpret nature's meaning. The conclusions of cultural anthropology, for example, can usefully refute the claim that single-family dwellings or private medical practice or familiar adolescent behavior are somehow "natural imperatives." Specific institutions (such as schools or prisons) can be shown to be unrelated to the survival of widely held values. In short, an open-ended, pragmatic approach to knowledge and action remains mindful of the conclusions of scientific enterprises which accept a means-ends distinction, concentrate on means, and treat ends as given. At the same time this approach subjects every conclusion to its own test, insisting that experimental action alone reveals to what extent some public policy, way of life, social structure, or individual character is need-satisfying, to what extent institutions and roles prescribe *needless* destructions of the self.

Accepting an empirical basis for a conception of society as a system adapting itself so as to facilitate its survival, a pragmatic approach views individuals as incomplete, multifaceted beings, as actors naturally given to posturing, simulating performing, playing, equivocating, innovating, testing, improvising—in sum, disclosing themselves to others.[8] Because such an approach values nothing more than role playing, mere playing, pure politics, it denies established conceptions of virtue and justice. Nevertheless, it does make room for structures appropriate not for man's being but for his appearing. Men are accordingly to be seen in relation to a structured field—battlefield, theatrical stage, or political arena—on which they govern their conflicting drives. The existence of such fields—formal configurations constitutive of man — allows for the expression of man's most basic need, his need to appear and to support others so that they will be able to appreciate the meaning of his acts.

To welcome this model of the expressive society and of political man is to direct attention to presently uncontrolled and unknown structures of experience. No doubt, political scientists might hesitate to face and esteem a model which includes unfamiliar, marginal experiences in their fullness, not wishing to see and discuss them publicly. After all, many of these experiences remain private and taboo, at most revealed to one's analyst in semiprivate sessions as privileged communication. Yet when enticed by an open-ended model and sustained by economic and psychological resources, political scientists may find themselves moved to expose currently repressed dimensions of themselves and others, expand political consciousness, and gradually establish those latent aspects of life which give men full employment. They will thereby do justice to human potentialities still in repose, still waiting to be exhibited and activated.

One ineluctable result will be the transcendance of ways of practicing political science that are not fully political, that are merely ideological. Sheldon Wolin has identified the point of departure:

> *Systems theories, communication theories, and structural-functional theories are unpolitical theories shaped by the desire to explain certain forms of non-political phenomena. They offer no significant choice or critical analysis of the quality, direction, or fate of public life. Where they are not alien intrusions, they share the same uncritical — and therefore untheoretical — assumptions of the prevailing political ideology which justifies the present "authoritative allocation of values" in our society.*[9]

To recognize how accredited approaches for coping with political phenomena merely complement the phenomena themselves, how so-called theories of political science are mere analogues to the prevailing procedures for organizing men, is to become aware of the ideological character of the discipline. It is to see traditional political science as partisan and propagandistic, as committed to the status quo. Once this becomes clear, it should be easier for the political scientist to welcome potential interests, to express his concern for more than the dead center of politics, and to begin to legitimate a reality transcending the present. He can thereby make political science a liberating discipline, one which demotes established political theories and political practices, one which moves him off dead center—a center which is *kept* dead by the prevailing machinery of politics and the alienating language and tools of political science, by its very definition of rigor and rationality. Appearing as a political being who is determined to establish more space and time for public action, he can make less of life private and more of it reputable.

Ceasing to distinguish between himself as political scientist and as citizen, aware of the way the distinction serves ideologically to deactivate and neutralize him, he demonstrates that his way of looking, talking, and symbolizing is itself a form of action. And he knows his action to stand in dialectical opposition to the prevailing way of looking, talking, and symbolizing. He emerges as a competitor with the status quo. Instead of adjusting his analytical schemes to the dictates of the nonpolitical world, instead of partaking in the conventional definitions of "decision," "cause," "efficiency," "politics," or "individual," he provides and tests his own definitions. Declining to serve and reinforce existing political frustrations, declining to purge his feelings and keep man's passions out of politics, he uses himself and his discipline to redefine the established structures of power, to bring more of political life—more of himself—into being.

VI

The Transformation
of Reality

We never simply know but always know something or other. Knowing is an active way of relating to things, but there are various ways in which the knower and the known may bring themselves into relation. When the knower assumes a detached role, he is engaged in no overt activity. He keeps his distance. He witnesses events, perceives what falls within his range of vision, and assumes a reverential posture. To engage in such contemplative activity is precisely what "theorizing" originally meant. By theorizing, so Plato maintained, we ultimately learn to see the universe as it really is. Beyond all appearance, it possesses some inner coherence, some essential form which the observer will grasp when he has become receptive to it. Keeping *his* desires in check, controlling his "lower" self, he will succeed in comprehending progressively more of reality. Such contemplation (which Nietzsche called "immaculate perception") will detach the observer from the urgencies of the moment and will gently move him to intuit that inner harmony of the universe which, once understood, enables him in turn to order his passions. In control of himself, his attitude toward the universe will be one of piety and awe.

Not surprisingly, Plato saw mathematical exercises as the appropriate character-shaping discipline for those who would presume to rule: contemplating the pure forms of geometry, prospective rulers would learn to resist the temptations of the flesh. They would not succumb to brute experience. They would cease referring to the here and now, to *this* object or *that* event. They would be moved toward timeless truth, toward ultimate reality. The purer, the more elevated, abstract, rarefied, and other-worldly the contemplated forms, the purer the beholder, for the less troubled he would be by the immediate, partial concerns of the world of mere appearances.

It was Thomas Hobbes who gave expression to an alternative way for bringing order to one's passions. Geometry is not the only purgative. One could also become tempered and responsible if one were to aim steadily for the satisfaction of human needs more mundane than the need to contemplate Plato's pure forms. That is, one might still do one's mathematics, but now merely to calculate the extent to which conflicting policies might satisfy the most pressing of human needs. To find out what these needs are, one would have to calculate and act. Admittedly, we already know of everyone's need for a life which would be other than "solitary, poor, nasty, brutish, and short." But beyond noting that everyone needs to assert and augment himself, or at least to defy the imperatives of nature, we have no authority for defining human needs. If, then, we wish to moderate existing passions, to bring the conflicting desires of the mass of men into some civil balance, we can do no more than seek to determine the consequences of our action empirically. This procedure — requiring a leviathan-like apparatus for self-control — yields all we can reasonably hope for; it facilitates what Hobbes called "commodious living."

To be sure, Hobbes's approach establishes no set of immutable principles, no abstract body of knowledge for ruling, no timeless code to which the good man conforms. It merely legitimates a method. Skeptical toward all positive conclusions, it merely argues for the uses of a process of negation — most radically enjoining us *not* to accept any universe simply as given. Implicitly, we are directed to rule ourselves and others, to act upon experience. And to do so as painlessly as possible, we must seek to understand how alternative policies might facilitate life, aid survival, promote "commodious living."

To gain such empirical understanding one must postulate alternatives and act on them. Theories, models, symbol systems, analytical constructs — all these are proposals for action, propositions to be tested. They are, as Dewey was to say, "plans for operations to be performed."[1] They have whatever meaning men are able to attribute to them. If we are to use mathematics, it must be used not as an exercise for elimination of the mundane desires of the "lower" self, but rather as an instrument to enable men to conduct their affairs more effectively, to enlarge their capacities, to produce effects and set up a peaceful, well-ordered commonwealth.

Knowledge in Action

This Hobbesian approach serves to vindicate man as creator of himself and his world, as designer of his morality and his future. It serves to free him from the grip not perhaps so much of Plato as of those who have had the power—in public life or in the universities—to tell others what Plato "really" meant. It destroys not ancient wisdom, I think, but the presumed wisdom of those who perennially inform others what Plato had in mind.[2] It deflates the notion that such elevated objects of our desires as Justice, Honor, Welfare, Peace, Pleasure, Wealth, Sanity, or Success are anything other than what we choose to name them.

Once our minds have been freed to redesign our norms and rename our experiences, we are empowered to act in accordance with our norms and our words, working to transform so-called reality. And as we keep relating to "reality" in this active way, we know how we have brought about transformations of its meaning. Realizing that increased knowledge is the function of our own ability to engage in transactions with our environment, we will persist in changing our relationships to the world about us, seeking to experience the world in ever new ways, multiplying reality for ourselves.

By engaging in such acts, the political scientist transforms the meaning of experience *while knowing what he is doing.* What he knows at that point is not, however, any environment as such—society as it "really" is. Nor does he know his own nature, his qualities as they "really" are. Neither he nor his world is reduced to unambiguously specifiable knowledge. What he knows instead —what he can make known to others—is the meaning structure of an experienced relationship: he comprehends the meaning of

95

the *relation* between his subject of inquiry and himself. Together, they constitute his field.

The symbols he uses to express his knowledge serve to structure the way he brings his ever variable self into relation with his ever variable subject. And insofar as he symbolizes his experience, thereby comprehending it, he can move others to share it. His field—the field encompassed by what I would regard as authentic political science—is thus neither some fixed space-time nor something *set* in space and time, but rather a complex, fluid whole which includes his subject matter as well as himself. And because both he and his subject can only appear in symbolic form, his field is necessarily one of a shared order of symbols, a symbolic community. His contribution to this shared order makes it possible to see it at any one moment as the fixed expression of the transactions among persons (himself included) who are continuously redefining themselves, who are engaged in an ongoing

> *Within the flickering, inconsequential acts of separate selves dwells a sense of the whole which claims and dignifies them. In its presence we put off mortality and live in the universal. The life of the community in which we live and have our being is the fit symbol of this relationship.*
> —John Dewey
> "Human Nature and Conduct" (1930)

interrogation, an endless test of their capacity to remain in re-creative process.

Whereas a positivistic political science provides firm points of reference, hard-edged contours, isolated entities, distinct decisions, and causal sequences, a transactional one leaves nothing stable other than man's capacity for creating structures which sustain experiment and change. As the observer risks vertigo and keeps moving, he perceives and knows things from ever new points of view, in an always different light. *What* he relates, he treats not as inert objects but as subject matter that might be ordered in an infinite variety of alternative ways. Whether he establishes physical contact with his subject matter or acts upon it only in imagination, he loosens it up: he sees it anew, turns it over, beckons to it. He approaches it expectantly, hoping to activate it, expecting it to become responsive, meaningful, and communicative in new ways. Treated in this way, the environment is made to lose its definitive, final character. It becomes pregnant with possibilities, unstable and suggestive. In Dewey's words, data thereby become "indications, evidence, signs, clues to and of something still to be reached."[3] Facts become potentialities, and what seems clearly dead to the observer determined to get a hold of manifest reality turns out to be full of promise for action, awaiting a life of its own.

Not only do the institutions of society cease to be something solid and autonomous "out there," but so do the ways men are conscious of them. Existing social relations as well as our unreflective awareness of them are deprived of their thing-like nature. In the awkward idiom of Marxism, both are de-reified. No longer accepted as existing independent of human construction, seemingly fixed occupational, sexual, and racial roles undergo a process of demystification. Once men perceive the entire complex of social and economic relations as dependent on and produced by them rather than as an independent reality, they are bound to question whatever abstractions presume to vindicate its independence: theology, jurisprudence, sociology, economics, and political science, all disciplined rationalizers of so-called autonomous truths about man and society. The result should be both disillusioning and clarifying. And when men can bear such clarity, they gain in personal autonomy and consent to be governed only to the extent that they have come to know externally imposed routines as indispensable to their own continuous development.

If we expect to comprehend not inert objects but situations constituted by men who are quite naturally disposed to act, we must treat the world as if it were always open to review and reconstruction. Whatever is felt to be inert, dead, brutalized, esoteric, reified, or devoid of potential for change — every closed

97

system—must be treated as properly a target for disciplined action. It follows that the proper activity of political science—of all men in politics—is the critique of false consciousness, the public review and reconstruction of closed systems. Oriented by an ideal of life as open-ended and as subject to continuous political reorganization, we can measure the gap between what we are and what we might be, between the present reality and future possibilities, between an alienated and an authentic existence. When this gap makes us sufficiently uneasy, we unavoidably feel moved to close it. Our ideal norm therefore does more than direct attention to our troubles: it induces us to act, to test environments in order to make them yield. It leads us to identify those aspects of our environment which are most oppressive, to locate and bring to the center of attention all arrangements which keep us frustrated, alienated, privatized, nonpolitical, all institutions which needlessly limit our actions and undercut our promise. Our norm compels us to focus, as Marx wrote, on "all relationships in which man is humbled, enslaved, abandoned, despised."[4] Precisely because the arrangements and relationships which prevent man from developing his potentialities are nonpolitical, they become fair game for all who have the will to act—not excluding action-oriented political scientists.

It should not be hard to see, I think, that political science —its organization, concepts, conventions, publications—might itself be a block to responsible action, and might therefore be a proper target for critical review and experimental reconstruction. As a knowledge industry, as a merely human contrivance or social movement, it too may set elite-serving deadlines, being something less than a *political* science. Its strategies, procedures, and educational practices may contribute to the maintenance of closed systems. Insofar, then, as it fails to give status to propositions which multiply meanings, political science—each political scientist—must confront not only nonpolitical environments but also its own practices. It must locate self-imposed obstacles to giving names to experience and expose needlessly accepted inhibitions to action. Distinctions which keep political scientists from becoming professionally effective—from becoming politically active—must be put in jeopardy. When experience shows, for example, that the acceptance of the conventional distinctions between fact and value, theory and practice, public and private, knower and known, or scientist and citizen are not apt to promote a conception of man's situation as one of his own making, they must be characterized as harmful. They must be discredited when their acceptance leads to controls greater than political scientists need to bring order to what is properly their primary interest — widening the range of meaningful experience.

Political scientists are thus charged with disrupting whichever of their own operations and postures fail to support a conception of themselves and others as political by nature, whichever of their modes of inquiry lead to a conception of man as merely reactive and conditioned, as wholly absorbed by his social roles. They must challenge the posture of detached, condescending irony, or a research process which, indifferent to the need to comprehend their relation to their subject matter, treats its subject as object. In short, political scientists must challenge all nonpolitical experience, whether it is their own or that of others. By encouraging disciplined encounters with nonpolitical aspects of reality, by deliberately converting nonpolitical systems and nonpolitical modes of thought into political ones, they will as a matter of course create as much meaningful experience for themselves and others as they can bear.

If political science is to multiply meanings by opening closed systems, what are the relevant procedures, cognitive styles, epistemological assumptions, linguistic conventions, and theoretical distinctions? How is "reality" best tested so as to make it satisfy basic human needs?

The Transparent Writer

Before considering how interacting with phenomena is likely to promote social reconstruction, I believe we should remind ourselves of the limited uses of ironic modes of inquiry. At the edge of despair, near total resignation, men have always been ready to use the last available mode for remaining composed: they decide to assent to their experience and describe it as well as they can. Aware of the intractability of their life, not willing to change it and beyond consolation, they keep their balance by resolving to call life what it is, describing it (even with affection) as unyielding, as deadly. Taught by their pains that they are terminal cases, they escape panic, terror, and madness by becoming stoic, by suspending judgment and refusing to discriminate. Resigned aristocrats, they will at most muster what strength remains so as to give expression to the conditions they perceive because of their own interest in perservering an irreducible actors. Thus Alexis de Toqueville both faced and depicted the fated triumph of equality, Max Weber that of bureaucracy, Harold Lasswell that of the closed garrison state, Herman Kahn that of post-industrial managerial society, John Kenneth Galbraith that of the technostructure. Less dramatically, American survey research centers have provided an image of an electorate of voters who are forever put-upon, the kind of miserable if lovable characters found in modern fiction who, in the words of a literary critic, "are portrayed in terms of rather simplistic laws of psychological and social behavior, while their own consciousness is groping, penetrated by only brief glimpses of light. The field of vision is at the extreme of externality, so preoccupied by the superpersonal design of social and biological process that the agents within it seem mindless."[5] Removed from their authors' unexpressed underlying moral impulse, these accounts of fated institutions and manipulated individuals exhibit a capacity for fastidious detachment, for objectivity and disinterestedness. The posture is serenely nonpartisan. There is no interaction with the phenomena, no experimental intervention—only rigorous clinical passivity, observations made without hate or love. Because the authors are ostensibly uninvolved, writing in cold blood, they find it easy to recognize our fixations, compulsions, addictions, and limitations, in a word, our *behavior*. They remove us from ourselves—at least our active selves—and show in detail how little we amount to and how well we behave. At the same time, they reveal themselves as superior beings, as condescending to scrutinize facts. Their works betray what Emily Dickinson termed "a zero at the bone." Their very prose reveals their capacity for self-denial: *controlling* their sympathy and their rage, they display their superior power—the power of aloof observation.

In its most radical form, as Roland Barthes has expressed it, the ironic defiance of one's fate demands writing in the indicative mood without color or emotion, writing at degree zero, forcing oneself to climb above partisan conflict and emerge as so innocent that one's words become wholly transparent and lucid.[6] The voice is final and godlike — calm, clear, and invincible, showing no trace of the passion required to find it. Every sensibility is expressed in the language of the translator idealized by Walter Benjamin. As defined by Benjamin, the translator treats the original as awesome even in its most common aspects. For him, the marvelous, near-miraculous thing must be that the original has appeared at all. He does not see the original as useful, necessary, instrumental, or functional, as having some ulterior motive, or as intended to have an impact or make a point: "No poem is intended for the reader, no picture for the beholder, no symphony for the listener." Creative acts are not *for* anything. And to make them accessible to others, they must be so translated as to save the *way* they signify, not to proclaim *what* they signify. Accounts of the works of others must "lovingly and in detail incorporate the original's mode of significance, thus making both the original and the translation recognizable as fragments of a greater language." What an original, a creation, an act *is*, may accordingly not be found in its message or point, not in the information it yields, but rather in its distinctive

> *Often I imagine a tribunal questioning me:*
> *"What about it? Are you really in earnest?"*
> *Then I should have to admit: "No, not*
> *altogether, I think far too much of artistic*
> *matters, of what profits the theater, to be*
> *entirely serious about the political."*
> —Bertolt Brecht to Walter Benjamin (July 1934)

way of existing, in its style and bearing. What the translator publicly ponders and celebrates is its specific appearance, the form in which it appears in his and our presence. His act is thus not one of categorizing, explaining, or even interpreting: it is but an act of illumination. "A real translation," as Benjamin defines the ideal, "is transparent; it does not cover the original, does not block its light, but allows the pure language, as though reinforced by its own medium, to shine upon the original all the more fully."[7]

Transcending Irony

Yet an exclusive commitment to the mode of the translator — an understandable temptation for political scientists who aspire to gain composure or status by separating emotion from fact — cannot be justifiable unless intervention is futile and absolutely no alternative action can satisfy man's essential needs. Only during truly desperate times is anyone entitled to accept the ironic posture and exercise what freedom for action remains by calmly describing the evils he takes to be necessity. He may then observe and leave a record. When nature (or the state) is implacable and his end is certain to be near, that is after all the only way to leave his own distinctive mark. Irony allows him to declare that he was around, he bore witness, he *met* deadlines. This may strike him as insufficiently constructive, being so obviously disproportionate to the revolutionary activities the times — any times — seem to call for. Yet when work which is constructive and well done turns out to be deadly, ironic forms would seem to have their uses. To *do* little, to imply only that there is a future which can redeem the present, to remain dramatically expectant, to remain visibly alert to possibilities, to give continuous expression to a posture of anticipation — all this may not be the least honorable form of action. Moreover, anticipatory gestures may also be seen as confessions of present ignorance. Admitting the precariousness of confirmed empirical knowledge and not wanting to count on it, knowing that the sources of redemption are not yet known, one can imply that the spaces and silences ahead are full of unshaped promises. In short, there may be times when one can do worse than project empty frameworks.

Yet when it does remain possible to do more for oneself — to perform acts of greater density and more weight — resignation is no less stamped with pathos for being deliberate. To learn what additional possibilities for action remain, there is no alternative to experimenting, to pretending that it is safe to give shape to the future, to doing *original* work, to acting as if one were free and paying the price if one's hypothesis does prove to be wrong. Guarded probing of reality may show what options remain open, the extent to which one's needs — most basically the need to amplify one's existence and communicate — may still be satisfied. When opportunities for experimental action exist, the warrant for irony is lost. Men are then obliged (not by some abstraction but by their own need) to risk some loss in composure and begin to integrate the role of observer and actor, of scientist and citizen. They are then obliged to join ethics to policy, norms to facts, and theory to practice.

Such integration is manifest whenever the political scientist—or anyone—interacts with what are felt to be ungoverned, nonpolitical forces of life. Acting to compel reality to accommodate the ideal of political man, the political scientist learns to what extent practices and institutions commonly alleged to be real are in fact changeable, to what extent his environment is more yielding than he thought (or has been instructed to think). He then realizes (in both senses of the word) the dimensions of politics—knowing *and* actualizing political life. His action will necessarily have the effect of jeopardizing the variety of his present commitments—whether it is a commitment to a functional division of labor, to the distinction between private and public sectors, to the system of fixed social and biological roles within hierarchical organizations, to government by a plurality of elites, to the market economy, to the identification of security with military power, to the separation of means from ends, or to the repression of action and pleasure, of politics and play.

At bottom, such activism challenges existing structures of power, seemingly fated superior-subordinate relationships. It questions the power relations established in schools, prisons, hospitals, academic departments, professional associations, political parties, industrial plants, and nation-states. Opposing an ideal norm to empirically confirmed experience, it makes targets out of the imposing social structures defined by a nonexperimental, nonpragmatic, positivistic science. Accordingly, an activistic political science is moved to interact with whatever organization of life the powerful insist is given—given by providence, the process of history, the necessities of industrialism, the iron law of oligarchy, the immutable nature of man, or the conclusions of social science.

Given structures of power (and the ideologies that sustain them) emerge as incomplete the moment political scientists include themselves in the field of inquiry, injecting their own distinctive interest in extending politics. Their subject matter is no longer simply given when they play the role Maurice Natanson has ascribed to the philosopher who "is not just one among many objects in his world; he is a prime object, the condition for the possibility of there being objects at all." As questioner, he locates himself "as part of the questionable and also as the source of questions." His questioning

> presupposes what might be termed a fundamental dubiety; it emerges over and against a ground of what was hitherto taken for granted. In raising a question the philosophic questioner calls into focus for the first time the reality of the object as object, the nature of the given in experience as given. The questionable is the object of experience taken as "strange." As long as we live in the world within the mesh of its familiar lines, the object remains only potentially questionable. The philosophic act consists in the recognition of the potentiality of the object and the liberation of its presentative force.[8]

Enlarging the field of inquiry by placing their interests deliberately within it, political scientists express promises which have in fact been denied. Detached from its conventions — its wisdom, its knowledge — they can free its potentialities, acting to represent what lies dormant. Like the novelist, they are able to express (in Alfred Kazin's words, which refer to Saul Bellows) "the texture, the vibration, the extremity of experiences." Where men generally are "too conventional in intelligence, too conformist, even too terrified," political scientists can bring their "intelligence, independence, and terror" into their work, giving experience a wider setting, a more refined consciousness.[9] Like the psychologist — R. D. Laing most dramatically — they change the individual's frame of reference. They thereby create new characters and types, new balances of interests. Their work thus makes conventional "reality" appear more incongruous, grotesque, pathetic, or comic than it does to the individuals enmeshed within it. When successful, they will have deprived the world of its normalcy.

VII

Political Science as a Form of Action

There simply is no way of getting it all in, and (except for that first day which may yet return) there never was. Even when the times seem to be uneventful and life goes on in expected ways, the distinctive qualities of our routines are never completely expressed by the forms we design to hold them. The drift of events is never wholly intelligible. Yet knowing this can hardly reconcile us to the inexplicable present. After all, this is *our* moment in history, or at least potentially ours. And we know that the familiar films, novels, poems, posters, songs, plays, case histories, and documentaries—not to speak of the formulations of the social sciences—have scarcely encompassed the contemporary situation, the impersonal, undesigned, still incommensurable outputs of large-scale bureaucracies—emissions, discharges, and excretions, the unprecedented accidents, miseries, disasters, and malignancies of the present. What we confront today would seem to be thoroughly baffling and unnerving, pushing us to the edge. To avoid hysteria or paralysis, we move toward the occult, toward silence and mysticism, rock and acid, away from *this* world, escaping the community and communication, finally shying away from all structure so as to embrace the unbounded fluidities of unknown experience.

The available forms fail to hold us. Neither fiction nor nonfiction quite works; neither can straighten things out, relating the unrelated news of the day. If only there were motives, personally achieved motives, one could write dialogues, dramas, comedies, tragedies. But when acts are point blank, fitting no known scale, we cannot take their measure, cannot weigh and mark them. If, then, the present remains inexpressible, an effort to give it a redeeming form cannot convince unless it also shows the strain and failure of its author. He must reveal the unavoidable inadequacy of his medium, the inability of his art to contain experience. Accordingly, we cannot accept the *ease* with which, for example, Truman Capote, John Hersey, or James Michener accounts for the slaying of individuals—a Kansas family, the occupants of a Detroit motel, or four students at Kent State. An account of new experiences (or of new dimensions of past experiences) must be suspect if its structure does not appear to be awkward and groping, its prose smudged, the tensions of its author visible in his work.

Vicarious Experiments

There has never been much concern in social science with specifying procedures for making the work of its practitioners appear awkward, for impelling them to reverse their thinking (or change their minds) so that they are finally compelled to take note of new tensions and provide accounts so structured that they communicate new discomforts. For Americans at least, few models exist. One is C. Wright Mill's way of rearranging his files (and his thoughts): he claimed that he periodically dumped out his manila folders, shuffled his notes, and then sought to resort and reclassify them. More specifically, he supported a kind of permanent intellectual revolution. He urged:

> An attitude of playfulness toward the phrases and words with which various issues are defined often loosens up the imagination. . . Often you get the best insights by considering extremes—by thinking of the opposite of that with which you are directly concerned. If you think about despair, then also think about elation; if you study the miser, then also the spendthrift. . . Let your mind become a moving prism catching light from as many angles as possible. In this connection, the writing of dialogues is often very useful. The release of imagination can some-

*times be achieved by deliberately inverting your sense of
proportions. If something seems very minute, imagine it
to be simply enormous, and ask yourself: What difference
might it make.*[1]

The techniques Mills recommended serve to detach the imagination from confortable theories at hand, enabling us to gain what
Kenneth Burke (on whom Mills relied for his strategy) has called
perspective by incongruity.

To free ourselves from our immediate comforts, Burke also
suggested that we should dialectically oppose whatever seems

---

*Thus it became obvious to me that don Juan's
knowledge had to be examined in terms of how
he himself understood it; only in such terms
could it be made evident and convincing.
In trying to reconcile my own views with don
Juan's, however, I realized that whenever
he tried to explain his knowledge to me, he used
concepts that would render it "intelligible"
to him. As those concepts were alien to me,
trying to understand his knowledge in the
way he did placed me in another untenable
position. Therefore, my first task was to
determine his order of conceptualization. While
working in that direction, I saw that don Juan
himself had placed particular emphasis on a
certain area of his teachings — specifically,
the uses of hallucinogenic plants. On the basis
of this realization, I revised my own scheme
of categories.*

—Carlos Castaneda
"The Teachings of Don Juan: The Yaqui
    Way of Knowledge" (1968)

---

imperative, attempting to gain knowledge by viewing our situations from incongruous points of view. Using this technique, we
might ascribe some disreputable, ostensibly absurd function to a
smoothly working social system, inquiring, for example, how the

educational system of the high school functions to destroy creativity or how the behavior of the American Medical Association functions to preserve an economic monopoly. Positing goals contrary to acclaimed ones, we can begin to make sense of seemingly odd practices, revealing them to be ingenious and rational. Bureaucratic corruption might be seen as a wholly rational response to a prevailing system. Or what is believed to be a sensible, pleasing arrangement, such as capitalism, might be seen as self-contradictory and offensive. Nietzsche put it concisely: "First step toward sobriety: to grasp to what extent we have been seduced—for things could be exactly the reverse."[2] We are likely to hear new voices when we postulate that one or another part of a social system aims at the very reverse of "success," "pacification," "development," "health," or "creativity." We become sensitive to the anguish inherent in "the merit system" or "gracious living" or "nation building" by negating these phrases, by enclosing them in quotation marks. Postulating functions which have the effect of shifting our perspectives, we both outwit reality and expose previously unseen possibilities. We perceive new realities—lives *not* lived (or not lived decently) because of decisions *not* made.

When we expose the empty space in which potentialities might have been realized, we become aware of lost experience. We are reminded of what might have been. J. G. A. Pocock has pointed out how this procedure is promoted by the very structure of our language:

> *The prevailing language structure assigns to us universes in which we play roles; it does so without consulting us and in ways which we may very well find repressive. But on the margins and at the buried roots of language, there is a rich field of ambiguities, absurdities and contradictions awaiting our exploitation. By speech acts, other acts of communication and by acts themselves considered as communications, we not merely expose these to the satiric eye but use them to liberate ourselves from the life-styles imposed upon us. We act in ways consonant with language and yet unexpected; we reverse roles; we discover contradictions and negations; we set off resonances whose*

subversive tremors may be felt at the heart of the system;
and we discover roles for ourselves in the teeth of the roles
which language seeks to impose.[3]

Speech may thus be understood as a process which serves to en-large perception by enabling men to grasp and hold progressively more of life. To succeed in this, language must be deployed experimentally and playfully. Its terms and syntax must be common enough to provide a basis for understanding, a secure point of departure — but not so common as to keep others frozen where they happen to be. At the same time, language must be strange enough to detach others from their usual business — but not so strange as to make them either hostile or indifferent. Our affirmations, moreover, must be so formulated that they will be perceived as answerable. To provoke denials, they must be at least partially question-begging, imprecise, and equivocal in their design, always a barely noticeable overstatement or understatement. Accordingly, successful communication is punctuated; it provides for discontinuities, plans for interruptions. Our pauses and redundancies — all part of the *discipline* required for increasing awareness — allow others to catch their breath and collect their thoughts. In *Malone Dies*, Samuel Beckett provides the model: "I stop everything and wait." By waiting expectantly, by using language designed to give others opportunities to frame rejoinders, by encouraging counter-arguments, counter-demonstrations, and counter-performances, we keep communication alive in a community of participants whose horizon is extended insofar as previously unexpressed experience appears in public. To succeed in this strategy, our data must be so arranged that they will stimulate our audience — including part of ourselves. If we do provide informative facts — actually *say* things — this is merely to activate others, to appear to be important. Facts are but creditable markers staking out territory in which others might be creative, marking pauses that allow others to catch up, to make *their* bid for recognition, to formulate *their* experience. At our unattainable best, we provide only empty forms.

To disclose the dimensions of unformulated experience, it is not sufficient to call attention to generally visible phenomena and rearrange them in new patterns. At best such an exercise will

109

only display how technical competence can be combined with intellectual agility. If the range of human possibilities is to be extended, there is no alternative to jeopardizing familiar arrangements and valuations. What men feel within present social or economic hierarchies, what they claim *when unprovoked,* cannot be considered their final testimony. What men say they want is after all conditioned, as Murray Edelman has shown, by the structure of the existing decision-making process and by policies which emerge from it.[4] Surveys disclosing the manifest happiness of the citizenry cannot support the conclusion that all is well. We are consequently not justified in seeing men altogether from what they claim to be their own point of view. To let them remain unaffected, where and what they are, is merely to get the "ethnographic realism" of Oscar Lewis or the kind of complacency illustrated by Herbert Gans's account of *The Levittowners* – Lewis letting people speak for themselves and Gans using what he calls "a democratic method of inquiry [which] assumes that people have some right to be what they are."[5] Both acceed to so-called reality. Inviting reality to report on itself, they tolerate its unreflective responses.

The political scientist concerned with comprehending as much as he can bear (Weber's motive, as he remarked, for doing social science) cannot accept men as locked in the postures which are all too evidently theirs. He must identify (not for them, for himself) a larger context, an idealized institutional structure which enables him (not them) to realize that every existing structure necessarily confines *all* of us – not only Mexican peasants or well-managed suburbanites, not only outsiders or deviants who are easily sentimentalized (and reified) by social critics. To see men as unfulfilled and their institutional structures as closed, to transcend the sentimental identification with one's subject matter, there must be a vision more comprehensive than one sustained by the positivistic urge to describe experience with painstaking exactness.

The difficulties of attaining such a perspective are made especially obvious by Robert Coles's *Children of Crisis* (1967–1972), three volumes which consistently testify to the author's attempt to probe below accredited reality, to cut beneath the misshapen, ruined surfaces of the men and women he encounters.

Yet the promise to provide a record of the invisible wastage of America remains only half fulfilled, for Cole will not approach and embrace the concealed aspects of individuals settled in positions of wealth and power. His work does not provide accounts of the unseen expressions—the repressed generosity and affection—of the men on top, supervisors, managers, bureaucrats, executives, owners. It merely focuses on people categorized as exploited and poor, on migrants, miners, mountaineers, sharecroppers. Coles does not move himself to perceive the repressed aspects of the rich, their frustrations and defeats. He has no time (no research grant) allowing for understanding of the poverty of the affluent, of those who appear to be fluent and composed, who *know* they require no spokesmen as open and articulate as Coles. His work—so respectful of the powerless—fails to reveal the deflected passion of the powerful, himself included. Failing to come to terms with authority figures, unprepared to expose the underside of dominance, he cannot enlarge our understanding of that part of the structure of American consciousness which is manifestly potent and decisive. He goes to Alabama, seeks out the certifiably defeated, and permits them to tell us more than we are likely to have known. What he ignores are the certifiably victorious. They fail to touch or move him. Accordingly, we do not learn about the defeated parts of those who are conventionally categorized as successful, the price they pay for their so-called achievement, their success in suppressing parts of themselves and their country. As Coles takes account of the wastage in American life, as he perceives the country's bitterness, he scrupulously limits himself: he does not include the misspent hours, the sacrificed joys, of those in the seats of power. His stories touch his readers, but not so as to move them toward comprehension of the politically significant centers of the social structure.

Coles remains as easily in control as others who have refused to be unnerved by the larger dimensions of social reality. He sees—but no more than can be managed by the liberal imagination. He writes smoothly and contains himself. His point of view only approximates the one praised by Alvin Gouldner, that of the classical dramatists who wrote tragedy:

What makes them great is their objectivity; and what

111

*makes them objective is their capacity to understand even
the nobility of their Persian enemies, even the dignity of
their "barbarian" slaves, even the bumbling of their own
wise men. They do indeed express a viewpoint which in
some sense does take the standpoint of both sides, and
does so simultaneously. If great art can do this, why
should this be forbidden to great science?*[6]

Of course it is not forbidden to political scientists to become progressively less self-denying and to renounce fewer of
their potentials. They may well begin to include themselves,
their subjects, and their readers within their field of action, recognizing that at best they transform all three. They might attempt
writing prose which insinuates that all public achievements (including their own) are only so called, that whoever names them is
fallible, and that man's works are distinguished by virtue of having
authors. In view of the conventional demarcation of professional
political science, it is not surprising that there are few works that
give life to a transactional paradigm by shamelessly including the
author. Studies exemplifying what is involved are not abundant
in any case: it is the rare work which suggests that the author was
present.

The most obvious illustration is of course autobiography —
an achievement such as Henry Adams's *Education* in which the
author moves himself across historical stages in the third person
as but one actor in mixed company. Beyond explicit autobiography
are such diverse works as Freud's *Moses and Monotheism* (originally subtitled *A Historical Novel*), Dos Passos's *U.S.A.* (biog-
raphies, narratives, current events, and subjective impressions),
Orwell's *Homage to Catalonia,* and Mailer's *Armies of the Night*
(subtitled *History as a Novel, the Novel as History*). Kenneth
Keniston, Robert Coles, Kenneth Clark, David Riesman, Robert
Lane, Robert Jay Lifton, and Erik Erikson—their identities partially exposed—have revealed how their involvement with men
in their social-historical contexts can enlarge the significance
of a specific situation, one which includes both the subject under
study and the inquiring social scientist.[7] Their concern has been
less with people who themselves sought help or understanding
(after all, two of Erikson's research subjects—Luther and Gandhi

112

—were dead) than with using the opportunity for interaction to
enlarge the range of understanding. Theirs are efforts to engage
in what Lifton has called his own study of Hiroshima victims: a
"shared exploration—mostly of the world of the person sought
out, but including a great deal of give-and-take, and more than a
little discussion of my own attitudes and interests."[8] Erikson in
particular is a felt presence as he interrogates and activates the

> By systematically complicating all issues,
> stressing the defects and the excesses of all
> values, insisting on tension, imbalance,
> uncertainty, and contradiction as the essential
> conditions of civilization, and the source of
> both its glory and its tragedy—by ironically
> qualifying the great triumphs, and reverently
> qualifying the great failures, we may get both
> a richer appreciation of the poetry and drama
> of history and a clearer understanding of the
> fact, the "reality" that concerns social science.
>
> —Herbert J. Muller
> "The Uses of the Past" (1952)

young Luther or as he travels to India to confront Gandhi. Knower
and the known encounter one another in an open, developmental
situation which Erikson's work seeks to rescue, recreate, and put
to wider uses. Thus in *Gandhi's Truth* (1969), Erikson calls for
a new synthesis, a therapeutics which assumes that "one can test
truth . . . only by action which avoids harm—or better, by action
which maximizes mutuality and minimizes the violence caused
by unilateral coercion or threat."

Awakening Political Capacities

Erikson's own acts are his works—including their obscure
parts, their allusions and diversions. They are experiences recast,
a form of vicarious experimentation, a dramaturgical testing in the
mind, and, as such, one exemplary kind of political science. As a
model for action—whether it be a written work or a practical

demonstration—Erikson's work shows how political science can break up, complicate, and interfere with what is alleged to be real, how it can lead men to increasingly complex orders of existence by transforming their present situations into political ones.

The subtle ramifications of this procedure are revealed by Clifford Geertz's review of a book and a film that portray life in a contemporary North African village.[9] His account of Jean Duvignaud's *Change at Shebika* (1970) and Jean-Louis Bertuccelli's film, *Ramparts of Clay*, which is based on the book, is so precisely to the point, that it deserves attention and space:

> Change at Shebika *is the record of an out-of-doors teaching project of the sort so many American students are just now urging upon their schools. Duvignaud, then (1960–65) Professor of Sociology in Tunis, selected a number of university students—fifteen over the five-year period—to take with him, in small groups, a few days or weeks at a time, to what, even for North Africa, is a rather beaten-down, end-of-the-world village.*
>
> *The students were all New Tunisians—highly Westernized, highly ideological, highly urban. Only one had ever been south at all, and she as a tourist; and though ten had peasant grandparents, only three still had rural ties of any significance. The professor, a man in his early forties, was a Parisian intellectual struggling to reconcile ideas from Lévi-Strauss, Sartre, and Jacques Berque. Apparently without more than a superficial knowledge of Islam, Arabic culture, or North African history (it is not entirely clear from the text, but he seems not even to speak Arabic), he was animated by an intense desire to educate the Tunisian elite to the deficiencies of their own view of their own country. And, finally, the objects of all this hope and attention were a small band of impoverished share-croppers, plus their wives and children— about 250 people in all—fumbling with the shards of a dismembered tradition in a marginal economy deteriorated and getting worse.*
>
> *The object of Duvignaud's book is thus not social descrip-*

tion as such. He makes a claim, in a methodological appendix, to have produced a "total Utopian reconstruction" of Shebikan village life, invoking, among others, Flaubert, Joyce, Hermann Broch, and Truman Capote as models. ("If Balzac and Dickens were alive today, they would be sociologists.") But, in fact, his portrait of that life is anecdotal, unsystematic, and more than occasionally stereotyped.

Nor is its object directed social change. Duvignaud wants to understand how change occurs in a place like Shebika, but, aside from inflicting himself and his students upon them, he did not attempt to intervene in the villagers' lives. He is not concerned with drawing up plans or instituting programs, but with causing mentalities to alter — those of his students, those of the Shebikans, and, though (curiously) he doesn't explicitly say so, his own.

In this, he regards his micro-experiment as strikingly successful:

> *The five years that we spent in Shebika were, both for the villagers and for the researchers from the city, a truly phenomenological experience of change. That is, the fundamental mental categories by which each side had conceived of change, if they had conceived of it at all, underwent a modification directly as a result of the study. A project on change became . . . an example of change itself. For the phenomenologist, who argues that the conceptual reality that actors present is perhaps the most fundamental form of social life, this is a dramatic experience. A village which had lost . . . its collective identity, gradually became the subject of change and of a history, a history that lay mostly in the future.*

One student, angered by the "irrationality" of local customs, finds himself drawn, simply because the villagers are so evasive about it, into an investigation of the local saint shrine, and though he doesn't find out very much about it, he does find out a great deal about why the villagers are so determined that he should not. Another, a girl, breaks under the strain of resisting her father's wish that she advance her education in Paris, as befits the daughter of a nationalist hero and high civil servant, instead of scrambling about in "this scorpion's nest." A third is paralyzed by the gap between what the villagers expect him to do for them and what he can do for them, which is essentially nothing.

On the village side, the disturbance is even more profound. A young girl, an orphan servant, dazzled by the example of the girls from Tunis, teaches herself to read and dreams of going away with the researchers; but when she expresses the dream, the other women pronounce her deranged and crush her spirit. A picture essay on the village in a mass magazine, prepared by the team, finds its way back, giving the villagers their first look at themselves from outside and enlarging, rather beyond reality, their sense of their importance in the world. The men of the village, employed by the government to cut stone for what they think is the repair of their houses, stage a protest when they discover that they are cutting it for the construction of a building to lodge civil servants and gendarmes coming through on inspection tours. This was the first collective political action any of them can remember occurring in the village.

The students grew more "realistic," Duvignaud says, the village more "purposeful." The first threw off the technocratic optimism of the Tunis elite for a juster appreciation of the gap between political plans and social realities; the second was "called . . . out of a state of passive mediocrity and bitterness into a consciousness of its own existence . . . discovered its own identity, and . . . the expectation of change grew sharper and more impatient than ever." Thus, microscopically and tentatively, was begun the process of inner transformation that, generally and decisively, will have to occur if Tunisia is to become what it pretends to be, dynamic . . .

It is a powerful picture, this bringing to earth of the children of privilege and stirring the life of a sleeping village;

116

and the picture is sensitively and imaginatively drawn as Duvignaud searches through the fine details of events for the faintest traces of dynamism. But is it true? Are the changes real, the dynamism genuine? Or has sentiment born of commitment merely made it seem so? Interestingly, the film Ramparts of Clay *suggests that Duvignaud himself may not be so sure. For the film, tracing over some of the same events, gives a picture not of inner dynamism and purposeful change, but of passing, quite ordinary tremors in a fundamentally immobilized society.*

In the film, the presence of the researchers has disappeared altogether. Shebika is rendered as hermetic and self-absorbed. The orphan girl's rebellion, the stonecutters' protest, the disappearance of a lone salt digger in the mountains are presented imagistically—the old women spattering the girl's face with sheep blood; the stonecutters standing up after three days of soundless protest to reveal the corpses among them; the horse of the salt gatherer returning alone. They are mere occurrences in a basically steady flow of life, like those small whirls of dust that are always blowing up for a few seconds in the steppe and then, as suddenly, dissolving. The rhythm of the film is largo, the angle of vision external, as from the helicopter shown photographing the girl dissolving into the steppe as it rises out of Shebika in the final scene. Even the alteration of title suggests the reversal of emphasis on fixity and a closed-in quality from openness and change.

The film is beautifully done, greatly courageous in its determination to risk boring most people for the sake of informing a few. Nor is it, finally, so much a contradiction of the book from which it was developed as a part of it, a complement to it. Diary and tableau comprise, in a sense, a single work. This is one movie where you must also read the book, not only on the pain of mere incomprehension, because the film is made in a kind of pictorial shorthand, but because together they suggest, better than anything else I know, not only how difficult it

117

is to understand North African society, but some of the paradoxes that understanding must contrive to contain.

For that society is both full of motion and also barely moving. And, willing as very few sociologists are to experiment with forms of representation, Duvignaud, powerfully aided by Bertuccelli, has managed, for all his limitations as a scholar, to make us see precisely this.

Geertz's review is full testimony to the promise of projects which include the self-reflective social scientist within the field of inquiry. Such enterprises, the review makes clear, violate old balances of interest and establish new ones—not, to be sure, in the space-time accessible to a political science recording overt behavior but in the minds of those affected. It does not matter finally whether the project is carried out between the covers of a book, on reels of film or tape, or, as in the case of a North African village, in physical space. All that is essential is that what Geertz calls "forms of representation" be so invitingly offered that inert auditors and spectators are themselves moved to enter the political field, to experiment, and to learn.

When our designs, constructions, settings, or acts are sufficiently evocative—sufficiently moving—they serve to *remind* men of unused capacities. "Ultimately," Nietzsche noted, "nobody can get more out of things, including books, than he already knows. For what one lacks accesss to from experience one will have no ear." Nietzsche asks us to imagine an extreme case, a book speaking of nothing but events that lie altogether beyond any frequent or even rare experience. Such a book, he says, will offer "the first language for a new series of experiences. In that case, simply nothing will be heard, but there will be the acoustic *illusion* that where nothing is heard, nothing is there."[10] Yet there is the frame created by the author in the desperate hope that conceivably it will stimulate a reader to discover aspects of experience, to discover them not in the book (which merely evokes) but through the book in himself—in that self the author shares with his reader.

I realize that such an equalitarian faith—hope for unborn or distant readers (other selves)—may be misplaced. The framework which provides the illusion that something is there—something real enough for the author who has realized it—may not in fact enable tired auditors to find their voice. It may not arouse interests which lie dormant. But I know of no way to find out without taking the risk.

The first step toward a community of equals may well be modest, aimed simply at enlarging the circle of one's peers. The author might follow Wayne Booth and assume he has power to transform whatever readers (or students or teachers) he might have, treating them experimentally as if they, like him, were able to make more of life real, as if they too were subject to change:

> *The author makes his readers. If he makes them badly— that is, if he simply waits, in all purity, for the occasional reader whose perceptions and norms happen to match his own, then his conception must be lofty indeed if we are to forgive him for his bad craftsmanship. But if he makes them see what they have never seen before, moves them into a new order of perception and experience altogether— he finds his reward in the peers he has created.*[11]

Ideally, the author's performance will result in an equalitarian society whose members appreciate one another's work. Having found appreciative readers, having successfully engaged and activated others, the author will have raised them to his level. Responding to his need for fellow players, he solves a problem far less parenthetical than Roland Pennock has allowed: "Rules of games are arbitrary in the sense that anyone can make up a game with whatever rules he likes. (Whether he will find players is of course another question.)"[12] Having fellow players is precisely what it's all about.

Although the author is moved by his need for participants, he does not strive to improve others for their sake. His is the more defensible motive that he needs others of equal stature to give credence to himself so as to grasp and love his own projects. At best, then, he will seek to publish for his sake, not his readers': he knows them and their interests to be a necessary part of him and his interests. Treating others as prospective equals, he will be less at war with his various selves, less punitive in his relations with the underdeveloped, illiterate, and listless parts of his world.

119

Society as Crucible

There is certainly no reason for political scientists to confine their activities to literary work. Physical spaces are no less stages for symbolic action. Ever since Machiavelli pointed the way, the political scientist has in principle been prepared to treat societies, too, as artificial creations, quite deliberately designing them so that they might maximize opportunities for developing his capacities, so that man-made institutions might generate as much variety and conflict as he can bear without being overwhelmed.

If his familiar environment fails to enliven him—if it strikes him as inert, dull, fatuous, or torpid—he is rightly impelled to become the author of more complex social enterprises, rearranging society, doing violence to it by probes, tests, irritating questionnnaires, and disconcerting research designs until it provides him with more stimulating material. Violating and restructuring social settings, creating synthetic spaces for experimental purposes, he in effect encourages new things to happen in what had been stable, well-managed enclaves—whether these are welfare bureaucracies, university departments, or professional associations.

Experimental probing can begin modestly at the very places political scientists find themselves at work—their classrooms, departments, institutes, or colleges. When these arenas are treated lightly—as if nothing achieved in them had quite amounted to what is proclaimed by course descriptions or catalogue prose, as if they held unfulfilled promises for participation—they are saved from easy success. Their incompleteness becomes public knowledge. And when projects to widen a political arena are accompanied by progress reports, the effect will be to provide practical demonstrations of theoretical possibilities.

Such projects would follow Marx's program to make every prevailing pressure "still more pressing by adding to it a consciousness of the pressure." The embarrassment of facing an existing situation—an embarrassment because the situation fails to live up to its promise—"must be made still more embarrassing by making it public."[13] In this view of the activities of political science, the practitioner *expresses* what he is doing. He does not

120

treat his operations as mere "background": his purpose is not to bring about some ideal end, a situation to put the mind at ease and the body at rest. Rather, it is to increase public knowledge of public possibilities in the very process of public action. He expects to fuse theory and practice, knowledge and action. Aware of his operations, seeing them as others might so as to be able to communicate this experience, he uses words to frame the world, to control the mindless forces of nature and society. Giving a running account of his transactions, he confers meaning on them. He thus makes new experience accessible to himself and to others. In a word, he politicizes it.

The least extensive intervention to politicize an environment—and the most refined—is that exemplified by conventional psychoanalysis. The analyst, always aware of himself, recognizes that his patient is in need of help, though not capable of giving a full account of himself and his needs. Psychotherapeutic encounters are therefore so structured as to free the patient to know himself more fully, to identify previously unexpressed and unused dimensions of himself. As Freud saw the process which impels

> *The transactional is in fact that point of view which systematically proceeds upon the ground that knowing is co-operative and as such is integral with communication.*
>
> — John Dewey and Arthur F. Bentley
> "Knowing and the Known" (1949)

both patient and doctor to become increasingly aware of themselves, its aim is "to strengthen the ego, to make it more independent of the superego, to widen its field of perception and enlarge its organization so that it can appropriate fresh portions of the id."[14] The therapist's role, and in the end the patient's as well, is essentially that of the participant-observer. Conventionally, when the social scientist acts as participant-observer, he is barely present. He seeks to remain passive, intent merely on discovering and registering what is there, letting subjects be and speak for themselves. In his case study, he ultimately relates what he has experienced, treating facts as symbols, as indicators giving him "insights" into partially invisible realities.[15] What may yet be done, however, to enlarge the conventional role of the participant-observer has been shown by Harold Garfinkel, who calls his technique "ethnomethodology." To shock men into an awareness of the tacit understandings and rules which *cement* society, he asks social scientists (his own students) deliberately to ignore what men take for granted. The ethnomethodologist is to pretend, for example, that he simply does not understand a most ordinary situation. Presuming to be an outsider, openly establishing himself in opposition, he will ultimately elicit responses which show bewilderment, embarrassment, and uncertainty among those in his field of inquiry. He violates the norms of others. The result is hardly surprising: "Quarrelling, bickering, and hostile motivations become discomfitingly visible." There is irritation, exasperation, anger, furtiveness.[16] Alvin Gouldner has aptly (if unsympathetically) compared Garfinkel's method to the staged "happenings" of the 1960s, pseudo-events designed

> to bring routines to a halt, to make the world and time stop. Both rest on a similar perception of the conventional character of the underlying rules, on a view of them as lacking in intrinsic value, as arbitrary albeit essential to the conduct of routine. And both are forms of hostility to the "way things are," although the ethnomethodologist's is a veiled hostility, aimed at less dangerous targets. Both communicate at least one lesson: the vulnerability of the everyday world to disruption by violation of tacitly held assumptions . . . It is a way in which the alienated young may, with relative safety, defy the established order and experience their own potency. The ethnomethodological "demonstration" is, in effect, a kind of microconfrontation with and nonviolent resistance to the status quo. It is substitute and symbolic rebellion against a larger structure which the youth cannot, and often does not wish to, change. It substitutes the available rebellion for the inaccessible revolution.[17]

122

I need not stress the risks in enlarging arenas for political action. There are possibilities not only of repressive backlash but also of bringing about unanticipated consequences—situations in which individuals turn out to be *less* free to develop.[18] The larger the scale of operations, the greater the risks, and the more care must be taken to keep the new political environments genuinely political, that is, open and experimental. If prevailing environments are to be disrupted, political scientists must take care that their own designs do not impose needless new constraints. They are responsible for keeping both their verbal formulas and their tangible structures open so that, like pregnant pauses, they demand participation. If the truth is manifest only in the completed whole (as Hegel put it) and if man is ideally never finished acting, both the historical stages political scientists design and their propositions about man's various performances must appear as open-ended fragments. The practical and theoretical structures of political science must be cast in terms which keep insinuating that human life can yet be lived more fully; its structures must make apparent the fragmentary character of whatever reality is being elucidated and actualized at the moment. Its practitioners, in other words, must feel impelled to invite distrust of even their own conclusions—indeed of all completed work. Their very tone must be that of the novelist, who, as narrator, has given up the omniscient voice. They must decline to act as authorities—in effect follow *Finnegans Wake,* which has been characterized as the first great book without a single sentence one can finally trust.

In practice, it is not easy to frame untrustworthy, vulnerable, ambiguous, open-ended projects—those which induce others to participate. Such projects not only fail to provide conclusions but also keep the future as precariously empty as Marx did when he postulated but declined to discuss arrangements for the classless society. Yet to satisfy the epistemological demands of a transactional paradigm, to make knowledge claims and future experiences conditional on action, there is no alternative. The past as known and confirmed is but a burden. What Marx called "the social revolution" cannot, in his words, "draw its poetry from the past but only from the future . . . Earlier revolutions required world-historical recollections so as to drug themselves concerning their own content. But the revolution of the nineteenth cen-

123

tury must let the dead bury the dead. In earlier revolutions the language went beyond the content; now the content goes beyond the language."[19] Because the language of the new is not knowable, political scientists cannot honestly respond to requests from instructors, project directors, foundation officers, or government officials who expect to be told in advance what it will eventually mean to create new political realities, what it will mean to expand the present and bestow political qualities on nonpolitical time and space. The political scientist must insist that he simply cannot *know* what anything would mean until the moment his resources are depleted—until his time is spent, his research grant exhausted, his life lived. He can merely display his past successes, make promises, and hope that others will temporarily trust him because they see how consistently he refuses to have the last word, to build an enduring structure, or to impose a final solution.

Criteria for Experimentation

The political scientist can win the trust of others by not threatening them—or, more positively, by demonstrating how supportive he is of *their* interests, how the pattern of their needs informs and disciplines his own projected activities. His controlling purpose is of course to make men's common life more elaborate and meaningful, to bring a greater range of human possibilities into public consciousness by dramatizing the nonpolitical aspects of present social and economic arrangements. To be sure, this readiness to have one's project judged only by its effectiveness in enriching life dismisses the array of controls to which the work of political science has been conventionally subjected. Declining to predict or even to explain, not claiming that the experiences he offers actually refer to experiences others have had, the political scientist will find it hard to have others accept his testimony. What will testify to the validity of his expressive acts? Why should others accept his equivocations, his fragmentary truths?

It should be possible, I believe, to recover and apply the oldest of tests, the one Aristotle applied to drama: he regarded a performance as successful insofar as it made the margins and polarities of human existence comprehensible, leading men to their fuller appreciation, inducing them to identify contradictory visions and interests which, when unidentified and merely felt, terrify and paralyze. The dramatist does not verify propositions but enlarges the contexts in which specific ideas and practices are seen. But he does more than merely display new heights or depths of experience; he also provides the forms which allow men to retain their composure while they learn to experiment, probe, and act. His forms — ranging from Plato's dialogues to the documentary theater of Peter Weiss — constitute a perspective which is valuable insofar as it includes the partial perspectives advanced by others, integrating (without eliminating) their narrower concerns.

By this test, an author is successful when his work establishes more parts of ourselves and our environment than we had previously dared to admit into our presence. The question is wholly empirical: does his mode of action move others to confront and incorporate progressively more complex realities? To the charge that he might simply lie, there is but one response, namely that he assuredly does, that at least so far the truth has not been told, that he merely appears to be truthful. What is at issue is not the fact that he makes things up — that his symbolic structures deprive "reality" of its success — but, as Nietzsche noted, the impact and quality of his fabrications. To what extent do his structures make a greater variety of experience manageable? Do they embody a maximum range of bearable interests? Do they serve to multiply meanings and create new possibilities? But there is a more demanding test: how ready are the symbolic structures to collapse once they have successfully appropriated new space and new time? Admittedly, they must be sufficiently firm and authoritative to shelter new experiences. They must inspire trust and provide comfort. But like successful psychoanalysts, they must not be so massively present and trustworthy as to make it hard to move on to new ventures.

Without claiming to be finally true, the newly established realities must demonstrate that previous establishments do not exhaust possibilities. To transform the prevailing structures, the new ones will have to compete with the old, challenging the political performances of the day — the acts put on by corporate boards, university administrations, welfare bureaucracies, National Guard units, peace research centers, or other institutions for crisis management. To compete successfully with the conventional drama of everyday life, experimental action—efforts to make counter-realities attractive—must enable men to feel the benefits of change, to experience the rewards of the expansion of political life. New reality-creating ventures merit support to the extent that, *without destroying self-awareness,* they lead men toward increasingly complex realms of being, freeing them to be

> *Any contemporary experiment in prose defines itself by the intensity with which it claims a form other than its own.*
>
> —Charles Newman
> "Beyond Omniscience: Notes toward a Future for the Novel" (1967)

progressively more playful and political, more active and alive. But the final test (one which might first be applied to student papers) must be its impact on the author himself: does the very process of ordering experience give *his* life a greater measure of meaning? Does his project dissolve old boundaries and enable *him* to gain access to additional dimensions of himself? Does it enlarge *his* respect for previously unadmitted elements of his environment?

VIII
Political Education

A perspective from which political activity is perceived as open-ended and value-creating serves so as to direct the political scientist's attention to the dead weight in our lives. Able to identify nonpolitical, noncreative, closed sectors of our existence, the political scientist can move more coherently to transform oppressively present organizational structures and attitudes. When such efforts avoid ironic detachment, they create new meanings and construct new realities. They may be practical experiments changing familiar situations or written accounts inducing both reader and writer to take cognizance of more of life than is immediately present. In either case, they demonstrate the satisfaction inherent not in achieving some end result but in being engaged in expressive activities. The final test of either of these provocative, intrusive operations lies in their power to bend what is alleged to be unbending, to expand political experience.

This test calls for doing what one can—not necessarily grandiose projects demanding unavailable intellectual energy. The costs of excessive ambition may require limiting the field of operations and engaging in what R. D. Laing has called "micro-revolutions." Without sharing his weariness, I would even have political scientists agree with William James:

> *I am against bigness and greatness in all their forms, and with the invisible, molecular moral forces that work from individual to individual, stealing in through the crannies of the world like so many soft rootlets, or like the capillary oozing of water, and yet rending the hardest monuments of man's pride, if you give them time.*[1]

Even such minimal action, however, may not be feasible: there are occasions justifying the belief (in Raymond Williams's words) "that if we move at all we put at risk every value we know, since *all* the actual movements, *all* the actually liberating forces, are caught up in a world of reciprocal lying and violence, with no point of entry for *any* sustained action."[2] But although specific defeats may teach one that this is the case, it should still be possible to define our political situations and make their pathos explicit. If one fails to live in happy times, they may nevertheless be partially redeemed by being generous with words and calling them what they were found to be.

To accept this flexible strategy is to welcome a mode of political science which does more than dignify the successes manifest at the center of public life. It requires a disciplined extending of oneself, surrendering hard-won methodological rules and current reality-organizing principles. It requires that the political scientist seek out and incorporate the flotsam and refuse at the periphery of consciousness. The proper procedure, as the looseness of my very sentences shows, is necessarily experimental and discursive, for it is possible to break boundaries and reach the unknown, unnamed territory only by discoursing, advancing ideas as scouts, sending words out to appropriate new worlds, using language to relate inchoate experience to established, well-formulated, and familiar structures. Acknowledging this use of the imagination to be a distinctive discipline, the political scientist should be able to move lightly and playfully through new territory, receptive to its promise, proceeding (as in life or as in this volume) in ever-widening circles. At the same time, he should remain prepared to retrace his steps as often as I have done, thereby avoiding more trouble than he can bear. Retreating when necessary, gaining confidence by being redundant, backflashing and foreshadowing, willing to publish variations of his themes again and again, he can ultimately demonstrate that the new territory is manageable, that it has been secured, and that the risks of moving ahead are tolerable.[3]

Dialectical Action

One familiar form of this procedure is that of a dialectic — the motion generated by efforts to contest a positive thesis, whether the thesis is a seemingly indubitable belief or a vested interest. To embrace a dialectical, reality-testing procedure is of course to commit oneself to the procedure itself—not to the antithetic side working to violate some established structure nor to the side so well established that its social origins have been forgotten.

The commitment to *both* in interaction, each dependent on the other, is scarcely apparent in contemporary political science. The conventional diction and organization of the profession discriminate against dialectical procedures by focusing on the static side, by accepting "politics" or "society" as if these were abstract entities rather than processes, as if they operated on men as independent realities. The entities are seen not as human construction but as reified systems from which men are alienated and which keep men in their alienated condition. By ignoring a conception of society in which men act as role players, by treating men as played upon by outside forces, political science is a party to but one of the sides of a reality-testing dialectic, not to the procedure as such. Moreover, it perceives the creative, reality-defying aspect of a dialectic as undisciplined and irresponsible. Such activism—willful and subjective and expressive—is said to expose its proponents to the gravest of all charges—that they are unrealistic.

To this charge, the best response is to acknowledge its force and not plead guilty. This entails not only affirming that it is all right to outwit reality but also demonstrating every step of the way that the escape from necessity, however agonizing, gives pleasure. It requires treating one's own work—indeed the whole of political life—quite seriously as a form of play.

Were political scientists to reconceptualize politics itself as play, they might find it easier to recognize the prevailing modes of analyzing and diagnosing political behavior as ideological, serving those who reserve the pleasures of play for themselves. They would be led to suspend their heavy rhetoric and attempt a lighter tone, risking ambiguities and puns, arrogantly (and playfully) speaking of political reality as if it did not exist, enclosing their most precious possessions in quotation marks— "the individual," "private property," "deterrent credibility," "the free world," "the democratic process," "the curriculum,"

129

"political science," and—why not?—"reality" itself. They could thus indicate that these marvels are only "so called," that they have made them all up and that—given wit and passion, courage and luck—they might yet remake them to suit themselves.

Agitating "reality," loosening the grip of "necessity," an authentic political science turns out to reveal what at any one time or place is unavoidably real or necessary—and what is but man-made and changeable. It thereby provides guidelines for enlarging control over nonpolitical realms of life. Indicating the possibility of alternatives, it validates the extension of the sphere of possible action. In effect, it therefore makes a progressively greater range of experience publically meaningful. Assuming that deprivation and alienation are forms of powerlessness, it arouses underprivileged aspects of "reality." To be sure, establishing political stages and keeping them in good repair is costly: there would never seem to be sufficient resources for allowing all men to make their appearance. Yet even when resources are scarce, political science can promote politics, encouraging at least the *circulation* of actors, activating those in the wings and deactivating those who have had opportunities to appear and are reluctant to let go—currently entrenched, dominant interests.

To engage in activities that attach and detach meanings, that make and unmake reality, is what it ideally *means* to do political science. Its point is not instrumental but expressive. The political scientist's concern is accordingly not simply with learning something from what he and his colleagues have done but with extending and intensifying the very process of acting. The rewards for him and his public come not at the end of the game — in the form of answers, results, conclusions, findings, predictions, explanations, or hypotheses confirmed—but in action itself, in the gratifying knowledge that one's ability to maintain one's balance under stress is being continuously tested—and that one has not, at least not yet, succumbed.

Requisites for Creativity

It is possible to appreciate such balancing acts by recalling that openness is a long-standing convention of empirical science—in fact characteristic of all institutions which reject

130

finalities by compelling men to review their conclusions, interrogate one another, and add to their burdens. The professional demands made by such a radicalized empiricism – one which constitutes what Herbert Simon has called the sciences of the artificial – are obvious enough. Committed to the openness entailed by esteeming man as self-governed agent and repelled by procedures and organizations which impose needless frustrations, political scientists are forced to identify practices and organizations which fail to serve man's natural needs – specifically his need to take turns in playing diverse, mutually incompatible roles.

As political scientists become sensitive to whatever forces arrest human development, they should learn to appreciate educational institutions which move men, in Marx's phrase, "to do one thing today and another tomorrow" without ever compelling anyone, if all goes well, ever finally to embody merely one of his various functions. Such educational institutions will serve to keep everyone in circulation, to make movements from role to role possible in practice, establishing a view of political science as a discipline supporting practitioners who place themselves in their fields of operation and who have the capacity to bear the strains of remaining there.

What should be clear is that the characteristics of such educational settings, of the practitioners of political science themselves, and of the institution of politics are at best quite the same, all manifesting life lived politically, each of them a sphere of action. Ideally, the polity is but the profession of political science magnified; and the profession in turn is but the individual political scientist writ large. Accordingly, suitable arrangements for the education of political scientists are nothing less than whatever arrangements can be shown to sustain the processes of political life as such. Whatever aids their political development, whatever practices promise to engage them more fully, whatever tends to enlighten and delight them further, should therefore be recognized as valuable. They must favor procedures which extend first their reach and then their grasp, which discourage backsliding, which enable them to resist the temptation to rest, to become fashionable or narrowly self-indulgent or visceral. To keep developing, they must be led to include ever more parts of themselves within their range of vision.

131

Yet there is no advance way of knowing what precisely would constitute the institutionalized ideal, how much exposure to diversity is required to stimulate political scientists to bring diverse experiences together and *hold* them until they are ready for more exposures and more integration. O. J. Harvey's formulation of the requisite setting reveals how little of concrete substance can be said about it:

> *To be maximally effective for producing articulated and integrated cognitive systems the input must always be* optimally discrepant *from the intra-subject baseline in relation to which they are gauged and assigned their psychological weight. If the discrepancy is too small or* suboptimal, *boredom may result, and if this should become persistent the subject may adapt to the situation of too little stimulation and subsequently react to novelty or deviant events with aversion. If the baseline event discrepancy is too great or* superoptimal *for the particular subject at the particular time of stimulation, avoidance of novelty and tendencies toward constriction of the baseline on subsequent occasions might also result. If, on the other hand, the situation presented to the subject is optimally discrepant it will be experienced as a positive challenge, will give rise to exploration and will contribute toward the system being articulated and expanded to include the previously deviant input.*
>
> *Of course, what is optimal stimulation or discrepancy for one subject might well be too much for a second and too little for a third. The idiosyncratic baseline to which the input must be anchored is not only a function of the breadth and depth of diverse exposures, but also is affected by native abilities of the organism and by the action of the training agent in connection with the exposures.*[4]

In less pretentious but equally formalistic terms, Leonard C. Feldstein has noted that men actualize their potentialities in settings that impel them to respond with "configurations of beliefs, judgments, motives, attitudes." If the configuration is too inert, "one responds stereotypically to new experience, alienated from some of his human powers. But should it be too fluid, one becomes amorphous and incapable of consistent and decisive action. The 'I' . . . is only fully experienced when the proper balance between fluidity and fixity is maintained."[5]

The requisites for development are settings sufficiently open and challenging to encourage the individual to become equivocal and multidimensional—to become not something definitive, merely a *person*. They must accommodate the self not only as acquisitive and achievement-oriented but also as generous and process-oriented. The problem, given currently existing organizational structures, is somehow to satisfy man's expressive, communal self, to provide educational contexts offering intrinsic rewards, and thereby to mitigate the effects of the merely acquisitive self and the merely instrumental organization. More fundamentally, to strengthen communal as opposed to individualistic tendencies requires support of what today are regarded as characteristically feminine roles.[6] It requires an environment sufficiently complex and diversified to make the playing of new and demanding roles a genuinely inviting option.

To encourage the development of repressed human capacities, practices and institutions which maximize the range of manageable experience must be injected into closed spheres of action—wherever men are noncommunicative and one-dimensional. The possibilities for converting private feelings into political acts have been more clearly shown in the arts than in educational institutions, finding expression in efforts to reduce the distance between spectator and art object as well as in efforts so to construct the art object that the spectator is invited to become an active participant—filling spaces, imposing perspectives, establishing connections.[7] The arts indicate how men can fragment environments by providing structures that remain open, that demand participation by the spectator, that transform passive spectators into active participants.

The New Discipline

It need scarcely be argued how this impulse in the arts can serve to reestablish political science. What properly consti-

133

tutes an education for political science is expressed by the classical proposition that an education for politics must be one *in*
politics. "Every habit and faculty," Epictetus observed some time
ago "is preserved and increased by corresponding actions—as the
habit of walking, by walking; or running, by running." The exercise manuals are abundant—ranging from the *Dialogues* of
Plato through Rousseau's *Emile* to the prescriptions of Dewey.

Were political scientists—political actors—to follow this
familiar (if unpracticed) educational advice, they would act in
ways commonly regarded as irresponsible. They would seem to
waste talents that (so it will be said) can surely be put to better

> *"Pull yourself together," you say? That's a*
> *good one. Don't you realize yet that I spend*
> *my life disengaging myself from my instincts,*
> *keeping them under observation, sorting*
> *them as they emerge, and then taming them*
> *for my advantage? Such is the discipline that*
> *you never manage to understand, the discipline*
> *that is entirely of my own creation, like*
> *everything I do.*
>
> —Jean Cocteau
> "Lettres à André Gide" (1970)

use, that might be brought to focus on some single goal. Yet by
accepting the argument for settings that encourage men to continue in action, they commit themselves to using the resources
they have within their power to develop. And they will finally
risk exhaustion, realizing that exhaustion and death are integral
parts of life.

We can become aware of the formidable obstacles to im-
plementing such a view by reflecting what it would cost political
science as currently practiced *to stop* its operations, to reverse the
dominant paradigmatic directives of political science, and instead
to make it rewarding to subscribe to their negations:

1. *Let convention be no more than a point of departure for defining the basic units of political inquiry.* While common sense and ordinary language are indispensable for engaging others, to *move* others, employ uncommon language. Define "politics," for example, not as a means to an end but as an intrinsically satisfying activity.

2. *Assume that the subject matter of political science is unavoidably variable and equivocal.* Political life is constructed by men in action, not by men who are unequivocally acted upon by forces outside or above politics.

3. *Assume that political life is constituted by symbols that mediate between the knower and the known.* Only when symbols integrate both aspects of ourselves is the world established as significant, as signifying experiences beyond immediate ones — that is, as political.

4. *Assess propositions by involving others and yourself in the process of testing, inquiry, and speculation.* Specific propositions — language acts — are *made* valid in practice; they are *realized* in action which includes others. Accordingly, research must be seen as an ongoing *social* activity less concerned with arriving at summary conclusions, judgments, or doctrines than with deepening and extending shared experience. Such activity entails accepting the fullest possible presence of the researcher in his field of action so that it will include his multiple unrealized parts, ideally his entire self.[8] One cannot *know* what is least costly to actual and potential human possibilities without involving whoever is affected by policy in designing society. The actor — man as at once political animal and political scientist — must therefore remain involved not in knowledge-accumulating projects alleged to be beneficial someday but in an inherently rewarding, reality-constructing activity which reveals *precisely* what one can successfully manage, what new reality can in fact be *made* true, what boundaries, laws, and promises can be broken without unbearable losses.

5. *Treat those parts of experience which defy comprehension as a functional system, using terms that keep you from acquiescing in its incomprehensibility.* Specify your terms in such a way that they generate disbelief, so that seemingly functional relationships may be perceived as dysfunctional and so that ele-

ments said to contribute to the maintenance of the whole may be perceived as contributing to its decay. Statements of experience must test and disrupt given states by implying unstated dimension. The intensity of the light brought to bear on seemingly hard and fast data must give intimations of what remains to be seen by men with more energy, more nerve, more vision.

6. *Define men as actors whose conduct—whose movement through time and space—is self-reflective and self-determined.*

7. *Seek to understand political phenomena by empathic acts.* To comprehend the world of politics, treat events, decisions, and situations so that they appear to be complete in themselves, irreducibly, incomparably, unspeakably unique—and continuously acknowledge your inability to succeed by pretending that you are making comparisons, establishing correlations, ascribing causes, and attributing functions.

8. *Regard your formulations as always incomplete acts.* Formulate your speech acts, verbal performances, and public demonstrations so that others are led to add to them.

9. *Express yourself in terms no more clear than you must to win and hold others.* Let your terms be as ambiguous as you judge others are able to stand, risking nonrecognition and oblivion.

10. *Accept procedures—constraining practices—which facilitate continuous expression and lead to increasingly ambiguous formulations.* Reinforce whatever enables you to remain ambivalent toward procedures, institutions, and rules which have been found useful for leading men to act, which are mere means. This should keep them from becoming entrenched as autonomous ends.

11. *Work on problems set by your need to give shared meanings to transactions with seemingly intransigent nonpolitical environments.*

12. *Welcome whatever clues for reality-expanding action are offered by other reality-constructing communities.* Take part in the plays of others.

Admittedly, these directives prescribe no definitive course of action. They tell no one when he has arrived, only how well he is traveling. Because basically the political scientist is merely directed to keep moving and to expand himself by sharing his experience with others—all the while reflecting on himself in action—he must finally find it difficult to distinguish between the methodology of the professional and the code of the citizen. All political scientists, in the end, are to be loyal to laws that keep them from ending, that enable them to *remain* demonstrative actors, political men who have determined to keep making scenes and to keep performing.

This is no easy discipline. It demands, after all, that political scientists remain consistently ambivalent toward every institution, especially that of language, seeing each of their behavior patterns as contingent and expedient, as mere expeditors of political life, as valuable only because they enlarge the sphere of action, as never finally healthy or just, good or true. Such systematic ambivalence rests on a loyalty to nothing short of the unrealized whole, and therefore on a sustained skepticism toward the conventional distinctions between cause and effect, means and ends, subject and object, pleasure and pain, death and life. These distinctions must be seen as merely ideological, polemical, or instrumental—not as inherent components of experience. For the political scientist, experience—every flicker of a sensation—can issue but one incontrovertible command: be attentive, heed me, heed as much of me as you can get in. To argue the contrary is still to appear and call others to attention; it is to insist that one's contrariness be heeded. Ultimately, what one is to be attentive to is not any structure or boundary—no grid of categories—but the unspeakable, unsymbolized whole which makes manifest that to live is to die, that the process of dying, of suffering and pain, is intrinsic to living, that the schemes which divide life and enable one temporarily to hold it are indispensable conditions of life.

Without distinctions, without words—organizers as well as killers of the dream—the political scientist deprives himself of the chance to extend his experiences and to live more amply. He needs privation, discipline, suffering, and death, for their absence denies parts of life, parts of himself. Nevertheless, as long as there are intimations of life not lived, of experience not confronted, he cannot close himself off by fully committing himself to some known order, some established way of organizing his dreams and making them secure. He must flirt with death, treat each of death's agents—well-accredited methods, codes, rules, disciplines—as replaceable, realize that anything more than flirtation—taking reality *seriously,* ceasing to *act*—is to finish prematurely.

To avoid completion, therefore, the political scientist (all of us) must do at least as well as the preceding words have done, designing projects (himself included) that succeed by failing, that fail to end. His failure will be constructive and liberating insofar he shows himself to disregard even his most impressive findings, jeopardizing everything he has confirmed or merely stumbled on. This very posture will indicate that his trip was not forced on him, that it was no less serious for being finally pointless, that he had been willing to squander his talents en route. Because it says nothing conclusive *about* the world, his work will

> *Learning is a transformation of the whole person, as any action is; in fact as the ground of action it is the continuing, manifold transformation which makes us what we are.*
>
> —Marjorie Grene
> "The Knower and the Known" (1966)

offer his formulations, concepts, and expressions as an integrated part of the world itself. The point is made more precise by Wallace Stevens: "The poem is the cry of its occasion."

Determined not to amount to anything outside the interminable process of politics, remaining in action, the political scientist will unavoidably risk the charge that no one can tell what he really stands for. There is but one defense: like Sartre or Cocteau or Mailer, he can make clear that he stands for nothing—or better, that he will not stand for anything, but will do so conspicuously, *meaning* it every moment. And not minding.

Political Man: A Bibliographical Appendix

Health, maturity, and development as characteristics of political man are distinguished in Nevitt Sanford, *Self and Society: Social Change and Individual Development* (New York: Atherton, 1966), Ch. 2. Also note Frank Barron, "What Is Psychological Health?" *California Monthly*, 68 (1957), 22–25; R. H. Vispo, "On Human Maturity," *Perspectives in Biology and Medicine*, 9 (Summer 1966), 586–604; Marie Jahoda, *Current Concepts of Positive Mental Health* (New York: Basic Books, 1958); Sidney M. Jourard, *Personal Adjustment: An Approach through the Study of Healthy Personality* (New York: Macmillan, 1963); and Charles Hamden-Turner, *Radical Man: The Process of Psycho-Social Development* (New York: Anchor, 1971), Ch. 3. A portrait of political man, defined as "authentic," is sketched out by Amitai Etzioni, *The Active Society: A Theory of Societal and Political Processes* (New York: Free Press, 1968), Ch. 21.

Social psychology provides useful sources for conceptualizing man as autotelic, self-governed agent: Gordon W. Allport, *Pattern and Growth in Personality* (New York: Holt, Rinehart, & Winston, 1962), and *Becoming* (New Haven: Yale University Press, 1955); Harold H. Anderson, ed., *Creativity and Its Cultivation* (New York: Harper & Row, 1959); Fred I. Greenstein, "Personality and Political Socialization: The Theories of Authoritarian and Democratic Character," *Annals*, 361 (September 1965), 81–95; Harold D. Lasswell, "Democratic Character," in *The Political Writings of Harold D. Lasswell* (New York: Free Press, 1951), pp. 465–525; James G. Martin, *The Tolerant Personality* (Detroit: Wayne State University Press, 1964); Abraham H. Maslow, *Towards a Psychology of Being*, 2nd ed. (New York: D. Van Nostrand, 1968); H. A. Murray, *Explorations in Personality* (New York: Oxford University Press, 1938); Carl R. Rogers, *On Becoming a Person* (Boston: Houghton Mifflin, 1961); and "Toward a Modern Approach to Values: The Valuing Process in the Mature Person," *Journal of Abnormal and Social Psychology*, 68 (February 1964), 160–167; Milton Rokeach, *The Open and Closed Mind* (New York: Basic Books, 1960); Harry Stack Sullivan, *The Interpersonal Theory of Psychiatry* (New York: W. W. Norton, 1953); Robert White, *Lives in Progress: A Study of Natural Growth of Personality* (New York: Holt, Rinehart, & Winston, 1966); Tamotsu Shibutani, *Society and Personality: An Interactionist Approach to Social Psychology* (Englewood Cliffs, N.J.: Prentice-Hall, 1961), especially p. 503; Jeanne N. Knutson, *The Human Basis of the Polity: A Psychological Study of Political Man* (New York: Aldine-Atherton, 1971). An ambivalent account of man as open-ended is Robert Jay Lifton's "Protean Man," *Partisan Review*, 35 (Winter 1968), 13–27; a critique is offered in Marvin Zetterbaum, "Self and Political Order," *Interpretation*, 2 (Winter 1970), 233–246.

Historians of ideas have done little to trace the changes in the conception of human nature which have led to a modern view of man as self-governed. Montesquieu and Rousseau are treated from this perspective in Marshall Berman, *The Politics of Authenticity* (New York: Atheneum, 1970). Part II of Ernest Becker's *The Structure of Evil: An Essay on the Unification of the Science of Man* (New York: George Braziller, 1968) includes pertinent passages. A comprehensive survey is Kingsley Widmer, *The Literary Rebel* (Carbondale, Ill.: Southern Illinois University Press, 1965); see also Dorothea Krook, *Three Traditions of Moral Thought* (Cambridge: Cambridge University Press, 1959); and Bernard G. Rosenthal, *Images of Man* (New York: Basic Books, 1970).

For a discerning treatment of picaresque fiction which

identifies man as a being in process, see Stuart Miller, *The Picaresque Novel* (Cleveland: Case Western Reserve University Press, 1967); and R. W. B. Lewis, *The Picaresque Saint* (New York: J. B. Lippincott, 1959). See also the model delineated by Norman O. Brown's *Hermes, the Thief* (New York: Random House, 1947); political scientists might prefer to be introduced to it by David C. McClelland, "The Spirit of Hermes," in *The Achieving Society* (Princeton: D. Van Nostrand, 1969), Ch. 8.

Marginal men may be seen as essentially political in Georg Simmel, "The Stranger," in *The Sociology of Georg Simmel* (New York: Free Press, 1950), pp. 402–408; Thorstein Veblen, "The Intellectual Pre-eminence of Jews in Modern Europe," in *Essays in Our Changing Order* (New York: Viking Press, 1934), pp. 219–231; Karl Mannheim, *Ideology and Utopia* (New York: Harcourt, Brace, 1936), pp. 136–146. See also Lewis Coser, *Men of Ideas: A Sociologist's View* (New York: Free Press, 1965); and the suggestive discussion of liminal personalities in Victor W. Turner, "Myth and Symbol," *International Encyclopedia of the Social Sciences* (New York: Macmillan, 1968), X, 576–582. See also Leszek Kolakowski, "The Priest and the Jester," in *Toward a Marxist Humanism* (New York: Grove Press, 1968).

Preconditions for the emergence of man as a political being are the central concerns of the educational theories of writers from Plato to John Dewey: see especially R. C. Lodge, *Plato's Theory of Education* (New York: Harcourt, Brace, 1947). Everett E. Hagen has summarized studies concerned with requisites for creative personalities in *On the Theory of Social Change* (Homewood, Ill.: Richard D. Irwin, 1962), pp. 123–160. Determinants of personal autonomy, role playing, and innovative capacity are discussed by Frank Barron, *Creativity and Psychological Health* (Princeton: D. Van Nostrand, 1963); and O. J. Harvey, "System Structure, Flexibility and Creativity," in *Experience Structure and Adaptability* (New York: Springer Verlag, 1966); see also Max Bruck, "A Review of Social and Psychological Factors Associated with Creativity and Innovation," in Charles Press and Alan Arian, eds., *Empathy and Ideology* (Chicago: Rand McNally, 1966), Ch. 2.

Notes

Chapter One

1. See the Bibliographical Appendix.

Chapter Two

1. See Robert Paul Wolff, ed., *Kant: A Collection of Critical Essays* (New York: University of Notre Dame Press, 1968). Note also Werner Heisenberg, *Physics and Philosophy: The Revolution in Modern Science* (New York: Harper & Row, 1958): "Natural science does not simply describe and explain nature; it is a part of the interplay between nature and ourselves; it describes nature as exposed to our method of questioning" (p. 81).
2. See Ernst Cassirer, *An Essay on Man* (New Haven: Yale University Press, 1944); and E. Sapir, *Language* (New York: Harvest Books, 1955).
3. See Jean Piaget, *The Construction of Reality in the Child* (New York: Basic Books, 1954).
4. Benjamin Lee Whorf, *Language, Thought, and Reality* (Cambridge, Mass.: M.I.T. Press, 1956), pp. 57–64, 212–214, 222.
5. See especially Friedrich Nietzsche, *Genealogy of Morals* (New York: Vintage Books, 1966); and Karl Mannheim, *Ideology and Utopia: An Introduction to the Sociology of Knowledge* (New York: Harcourt, Brace, 1936).
6. Thomas S. Kuhn, *The Structure of Scientific Revolutions* (Chicago: University of Chicago Press, 1962), pp. 5–6, 23–24, 90–91. For a clarification of "paradigm," see the postscript of the 1969 edition.
7. Sheldon S. Wolin, *Politics and Vision* (Boston: Little, Brown, 1960), p. 9.

Chapter Three

1. In an unpublished paper, "Violence and Utopia" (1971), E. Victor Wolfenstein, University of California (Los Angeles), demonstrates how useful it is to apply Freud's "fundamental technical rule of analysis" to different contexts: the analyst must assume that what is relevant to analysis is hidden precisely in that aspect of a phenomenon which the subject declares to be a priori irrelevant.

2. For attempts to define what Albert Somit and Joseph Tannenhaus have called a basic consensus, see their *Development of American Political Science* (Boston: Allyn and Bacon, 1967), Ch. 12, and works there cited; and Francis J. Sorauf, *Political Science* (Columbus, Ohio: Merrill, 1965), Ch. 2. The consensus is most vulgarly exposed when summarized for precollegiate instruction, as for example in Leroy N. Rieselbach, *The Behavioral Approach to the Study of Politics: An Overview* (Bloomington, Indiana: High School Curriculum Center in Government, 1969).

3. See David Easton, "Political Science," *International Encyclopedia of Social Science* (New York: Macmillan, 1968), XII, 282–298; and "The Current Meaning of 'Behavioralism,'" in James C. Charlesworth, ed., *The Limits of Behavioralism in Political Science* (Philadelphia: American Academy of Political and Social Science, 1962), pp. 1–25.

4. *The Positive Philosophy of Auguste Comte*, trans. Harriet Martineau (London: G. Bell, 1896), II, 61.

5. Joseph Devey, ed., *The Physical and Metaphysical Works of Lord Bacon* (London: G. Bell, 1891), p. 389.

6. That scientists themselves have often misunderstood what they were doing is shown by Paul K. Feyerabend, "Problems of Empiricism," in Robert G. Colodny, ed., *Beyond the Edge of Certainty* (Englewood Cliffs, N.J.: Prentice-Hall, 1965), pp. 145–260.

7. Galileo, *Il saggiatore*, "Opere," 180, p. 232; quoted in R. G. Collingwood, *The Idea of Nature* (Oxford: Oxford University Press, Clarendon Press, 1945), p. 105.

8. There are probably no political scientists who believe that facts are cold, hard, and stubborn, or that facts can act independently to confirm hypotheses. The point is not that this notion is still entertained but that political scientists professionally behave as if alternative notions were neither useful nor credible.

9. There has been at least one serious effort to show how paradigmatic directives are being revised by various attitude and participation studies that recognize that explanations are based on something more than overt behavior and allow for unobserva-

ble intentions: Arthur L. Kalleberg, "Concept Formation in Normative and Empirical Studies," *American Political Science Review*, 63 (March 1969), 26–39. Similarly, Heinz Eulau has not only urged political scientists to discover the uniformities of behavior, to engage in causal analysis, and to eliminate "what are considered 'merely mental' phenomena." He has also maintained that, to explain behavior, political scientists must determine intended meanings of political acts. For an account of Heinz Eulau's vacillation, see John G. Gunnell, "Phenomenology and the Explanation of Political," a paper presented at the Annual Meeting of the American Political Science Association, Los Angeles, September 1970, pp. 25–27.

10. *Selected Writings of Francis Bacon* (New York: Modern Library, 1955), p. 480.

11. See, however, the criticisms collected in Charles A. McCoy and John Playford, eds., *Apolitical Politics* (New York: Thomas Y. Crowell, 1967); and Henry S. Kariel, ed., *Frontiers of Democratic Theory* (New York: Random House, 1970).

12. Hannah Arendt, "Lying in Politics: Reflections on the Pentagon Papers," *The New York Review*, November 18, 1971, p. 32.

Chapter Four

1. The Latin root of "fact" is *factum:* that which is done or placed. *Factum* is the neuter past participle of *facere:* to act or to perform, that is, to place what has been drifting.

2. Dynamism and irreverence are moved to the center of science by Arthur Koestler, *The Act of Creation* (London: Hutchinson, 1964); and James D. Watson, *The Double Helix* (New York: Atheneum, 1968).

3. Niccolò Machiavelli, *The Prince* (New York: Modern Library, 1940), p. 65.

4. Friedrich Nietzsche, *On Truth and Lie in an Extra-Moral Sense* (1873), quoted in H. S. Kariel, ed., *Sources in Twentieth-Century Political Thought* (New York: Free Press, 1964), 'pp. 5, 8.

5. Hannah Arendt, *The Origins of Totalitarianism* (New York: Harcourt, Brace, 1951), pp. 434–436.

6. Hannah Arendt, *The Human Condition* (Chicago: University of Chicago Press, 1958), pp. 198–199.

7. John Dewey and Arthur F. Bentley, *Knowing and the Known* (Boston: Beacon Press, 1949), p. 272.

8. Dewey and Bentley wrote that "we have no 'something known' and no 'something identified' apart from it know*ing*

and identifying, and . . . we have no knowing and identifying apart from somewhats and somethings that are being known and identified" (*Knowing and the Known,* p. 54).

9. From the Preface of Clerk Maxwell, *Matter and Motion* (1877), quoted in Dewey and Bentley, ed., *Knowing and the Known,* p. 106.

10. Anselm Strauss, ed., *The Social Psychology of George Herbert Mead* (Chicago: University of Chicago Press, 1956), p. 2.

11. See Friedrich Nietzsche, *The Use and Abuse of History* (New York: Liberal Arts Press, 1949); and George Herbert Mead, "History and the Experimental Method," in Strauss, ed., *Social Psychology of George Herbert Mead,* pp. 60–68.

12. William James, *Collected Essays and Reviews* (London: Longmans, Green, 1920), p. 67.

13. "If men define situations as real, they are real in their consequence." W. I. Thomas, *The Child in America* (New York: Alfred A. Knopf, 1928), p. 584.

14. Quoted by Isaiah Berlin, "A Note on Vico's Concept of Knowledge," in Giorgio Tagliacozzo, ed., *Giambattista Vico: An International Symposium* (Baltimore: Johns Hopkins Press, 1970), pp. 371–377.

15. Tagliacozzo, ed., *Giambattista Vico,* pp. 373, 375, 376. In his *Metamorphosis of Plants* (1790), Goethe carried this approach into the physical sciences: one could grasp the inner meaning of nature, he affirmed, by seeing "her at work and alive, manifesting herself in her wholeness in every single part of her being." Each part expressed the whole, but what it expressed— its inner structure—could be visible only to the mind. In his *Theory of Colors* (1810), Goethe questioned Newtonian empiricism and noted that "merely looking at a thing is of no use whatsoever. Looking at a thing gradually merges into contemplation and contemplation into thinking. Because thinking is establishing connections it is possible to say that every attentive glance which we cast on the world is an act of theorizing. This, however, ought to be done with consciousness, self-criticism, freedom, and, to use a daring word, with irony—yes, all these faculties are necessary if abstraction, which we dread, is to be rendered innocuous, and the result which we hope for is to emerge with as much liveliness as possible." (In Jubiläums-Ausgabe [Stuttgart], XL, 63.) How difficult it is to dismiss Goethe's venture as unscientific is brilliantly shown in Erich Heller, *The Disinherited Mind* (Cambridge: Bowes & Bowes, 1952), Ch. 1.

16. Cf.: "He who puts himself into the place of another's subjectivity and reproduces his experiences extinguishes the specificity of his own identity just like the observer of an experiment. Had Dilthey followed the logic of his own investigations,

he would have seen that objectivity of understanding is possible only within the role of the reflected partner *in a communication structure.*" (Jürgen Habermas, *Knowledge and Human Interests* [Boston: Beacon Press, 1971], p. 181; emphasis supplied.) See also George Devereux, *From Anxiety to Method in Behavioral Science* (The Hague: Mouton, 1967).

17.   The literature is complex and voluminous, but the following works are central: Wilhelm Dilthey, *Einleitung in die Geisteswissenschaften* (Leipzig: Teubner, 1922); Heinrich Rickert, *Kulturwissenschaft und Naturwissenschaft* (Tubingen: J. C. B. Mohr, 1910); Max Weber, *Max Weber on the Methodology of the Social Sciences* (New York: Free Press, 1949). See also Richard Taylor, *Action and Purpose* (Englewood Cliffs, N.J.: Prentice-Hall, 1966); John G. Gunnell, "Social Science and Political Reality: The Problem of Explanation," *Social Research*, 35 (Spring 1968), 159–201; Maurice Natanson, ed., *Philosophy of the Social Sciences: A Reader* (New York: Random House, 1963); Paul F. Kress, *Social Science and the Idea of Process* (Urbana, Ill.: University of Illinois Press, 1970); and Georg Henrik von Wright, *Explanation and Understanding* (Ithaca, N.Y.: Cornell University Press, 1971).

18.   This is not acknowledged in an otherwise astute analysis by A. R. Louch, *Explanation and Human Action* (Oxford: Basil Blackwell & Mott, 1966), Ch. 9.

Chapter Five

1.   Karl Marx, *Capital* (Moscow: Foreign Languages Publishing House, 1954), III, 799–800; the emphasis is supplied.

2.   William James, *The Will to Believe* (New York: Dover, 1956), p. 205. This valuation may be seen as at one with that of Hegel.

3.   Karl W. Deutsch, *The Nerves of Government* (New York: Free Press, 1963), p. 140.

4.   See bibliographical appendix for some of the relevant literature.

5.   *The Active Society: A Theory of Societal and Political Processes* (New York: Free Press, 1968), p. 626.

6.   Max Weber, *Aufsätze zur Wissenschaftslehre* (Tubingen: J. C. B. Mohr, 1925), p. 150.

7.   See Hugh Stretton, *The Political Sciences* (London: Routledge & Kegan Paul, 1969), pp. 226–228; and Oran Young, *Systems of Political Science* (Englewood Cliffs, N.J.: Prentice-Hall, 1968).

8.   This empirical basis makes it possible to determine which among competing policies are likely to promote adaptive-

ness, personal authenticity, and collective survival. See Peter A. Corning, *Politics and Survival* (New York: Alfred A. Knopf, 1972); Abraham Edel, *Ethical Judgment: The Uses of Science in Ethics* (New York: Free Press, 1955); Frederick M. Watkins, "Natural Law and the Problem of Value-Judgment," in Oliver Garceau, ed., *Political Research and Political Theory* (Cambridge, Mass.: Harvard University Press, 1968), pp. 58–74; and Amitai Etzioni, *The Active Society* (New York: Free Press, 1968), Ch. 21.

9. Sheldon S. Wolin, "Political Theory as a Vocation," *American Political Science Review*, 63 (December 1969), p. 1063. How precisely the practices of American pluralism square with the existing paradigm of political science is also shown in Bernard Crick, *The American Science of Politics* (Berkeley: University of California Press, 1959); Norman Jacobson, "Political Science and Political Education," *American Political Science Review*, 57 (September 1963), pp. 561–569; and Henry S. Kariel, *The Decline of American Pluralism* (Stanford: Stanford University Press, 1961), Ch. 9.

Chapter Six

1. John Dewey, *The Quest for Certainty: A Study of the Relations of Knowledge and Action* (New York: Minton, Balch, 1929), p. 138.

2. That Plato and other thinkers always had more in mind than *what* they said is worth stressing when we are tempted to neglect *how* they said it. See especially David Grene, *Man in His Pride* (Chicago: University of Chicago Press, 1950); Alvin W. Gouldner, *Enter Plato* (New York: Basic Books, 1965), pp. 166–196, 267–296, 379–388; Leonard Nelson, *Socratic Method and Critical Philosophy* (Gloucester, Mass.: Peter Smith, 1949); Stanley Rosen, *Plato's Symposium* (New Haven: Yale University Press, 1968), Ch. 1; and Jacob Klein, *A Commentary on Plato's Meno* (Chapel Hill: University of North Carolina Press, 1965), Ch. 1.

3. Dewey, *The Quest for Certainty*, p. 99.

4. Karl Marx, *Der historische Materialismus* (Leipzig: Kroner, 1932), I, 272.

5. Harold Kaplan, *The Passive Voice* (Athens, Ohio: Ohio University Press, 1966), p. 9.

6. Roland Barthes, *Writing Degree Zero* (London: Jonathan Cape, 1967), pp. 80–84.

7. Walter Benjamin, *Illuminations*, trans. Harry John (New York: Harcourt, Brace, and World, 1968), pp. 69, 78, 79.

8. Maurice Natanson, "Philosophy of Psychiatry," in

E. W. Straus, M. Natanson, and H. Ey, *Psychiatry and Philosophy* (Berlin: Springer Verlag, 1969), pp. 85–86.

9. Alfred Kazin, "Though He Slay Me . . . ," *New York Review of Books*, December 3, 1970, p. 3.

Chapter Seven

1. C. Wright Mills, *The Sociological Imagination* (New York: Oxford University Press, 1959), pp. 195–220.

2. Friedrich Nietzsche, *The Will to Power* (New York: Vintage Books, 1968), p. 320.

3. J. G. A. Pocock, "Verbalizing a Political Act: Towards a Politics of Speech," paper prepared for the Conference for the Study of Political Thought, New York, N.Y., April 3, 1971, p. 10.

4. Murray Edelman, *Politics as Symbolic Action* (Chicago: Markham, 1971). See also Isaac D. Balbus, "The Concept of Interest in Pluralist and Marxian Analysis," *Politics and Society*, 1 (February 1971), 151–177.

5. See Herbert J. Gans, *The Levittowners* (New York: Pantheon Books, 1967); and Marvin Mudrick's critique of Oscar Lewis: "Five Characters in Search of an Author," *Hudson Review*, 14 (Winter 1962), 630–634. Mudrick points out that Lewis's "realism" falsely assumes that the experience of the poor is equivalent to the words they speak into a tape recorder, that their "natural" language yields sufficient understanding of their existence.

6. Alvin W. Gouldner, "The Sociologist as Partisan," *The American Sociologist*, 3 (May 1968), p. 111. Cf. Walter Kaufmann's summary: "Tragedy invites people to identify now with this character, now with that, seeing the same situation in different perspectives and thinking about the relative merits of each. In this process our human sympathies are enlarged and extended to unlikely characters; we are led to question what in ordinary life we took for granted; we are made more critical, more skeptical, and more humane." (*Tragedy and Philosophy* [Garden City, N.Y.: Doubleday, 1968], p. 351.)

7. See also James Agee and Walker Evans, *Let Us Now Praise Famous Men* (1939); James Baldwin, *Notes of a Native Son* (1955); Maurice Stein, *The Eclipse of Community* (1960); Truman Capote, *In Cold Blood* (1965); Arthur A. Schlesinger, Jr., *A Thousand Days* (1965); Elliot Liebow, *Tally's Corner: A Study of Negro Streetcorner Men* (1967); Robert Canot, *Rivers of Blood, Years of Darkness* (1968); William W. Ellis, *White Ethics and*

Black Power (1969); Wright Morris, *God's Country and My People* (1969); Tom Wolfe, *Radical Chic & Mau-Mauing the Flak Catchers* (1970); Todd Gitlin and Nanci Hollander, *Uptown: Poor Whites in Chicago* (1970); and whatever works, including films, that succeed in making parts of the author visible and therefore vulnerable.

    8.   Robert Jay Lifton, "Psychohistory," *Partisan Review*, 37 (1970), p. 22.

    9.   Clifford Geertz, "In Search of North Africa," *The New York Review*, 16 (April 22, 1971), 22–24; emphasis supplied. Reprinted with permission.

    10.   Friedrich Nietzsche, *Ecce Homo: How One Becomes What One Is* (1908), in *Basic Writings of Nietzsche* (New York: Modern Library, 1968), p. 717; emphasis supplied.

    11.   Wayne C. Booth, *The Rhetoric of Fiction* (Chicago: University of Chicago Press, 1961), pp. 397–398.

    12.   J. Roland Pennock, "Law's Natural Bent," *Ethics*, 79 (April 1969), p. 225.

    13.   Karl Marx, *Early Writings* (London: C. A. Watts, 1963), p. 47.

    14.   Sigmund Freud, "New Introductory Lectures," in *Complete Psychological Works* (London: Hogarth Press, 1964), XXII, 80.

    15.   See Howard S. Becker et al., *Boys in White* (Chicago: University of Chicago Press, 1961); and for a general survey, see Severyn T. Bruyn, *The Human Perspective in Sociology: The Methodology of Participant Observation* (Englewood Cliffs, N.J.: Prentice-Hall, 1966).

    16.   Harold Garfinkel, "Studies of the Routine Grounds of Everyday Activities," in *Studies in Ethnomethodology* (Englewood Cliffs, N.J.: Prentice-Hall, 1967), Ch. 2.

    17.   Alvin W. Gouldner, *The Coming Crisis of Western Sociology* (New York: Basic Books, 1970), p. 394.

    18.   How unwittingly and insidiously social scientists can introduce constraints under the guise of freeing people is illustrated in Alexander H. Leighton, *The Governing of Men* (Princeton: Princeton University Press, 1945); B. F. Skinner, *Walden Two* (New York: Macmillan, 1948); and the experience with the Project Camelot as discussed in Irving Louis Horowitz, *Rise and Fall of Project Camelot* (Cambridge, Mass.: M.I.T. Press, 1967). Robert Rubenstein's and Harold D. Lasswell's *The Sharing of Power in a Psychiatric Hospital* (New Haven: Yale University Press, 1966) is a neglected success story.

    19.   Karl Marx, *The Eighteenth Brumaire of Louis Bonaparte*, in Emile Burns, ed., *A Handbook of Marxism* (New York: International Publishers, 1935), p. 119.

Chapter Eight

1. William James to Mrs. Henry Whitman, June 7, 1899, in *Letters of William James* (Boston: Atlantic Monthly Press, 1920), II, 90.

2. Raymond Williams, "Parting of the Ways," *Commentary*, 47 (February 1969), 73–75.

3. What this metaphor intimates may be understood as aesthetic education: see Friedrich Schiller, *On the Aesthetic Education of Man* (New Haven: Yale University Press, 1954); Herbert Read, *Education through Art* (London: Faber & Faber, 1943); John Dewey, *Art as Experience* (New York: Minton, Balch, 1934); and Herbert Marcuse, *An Essay on Liberation* (Boston: Beacon Press, 1969), Ch. 2.

4. O. J. Harvey, "System Structure, Flexibility and Creativity," in *Experience, Structure and Adaptability* (New York: Springer Verlag, 1966), pp. 63–64; emphasis in the original.

5. Leonard C. Feldstein, "Toward a Concept of Integrity," *Annals of Psychotherapy*, I (1961), 84.

6. David Bakan has collected evidence showing that women are not as achievement oriented as men, that they are less egocentric, more "communicative," less aggressive, less suicidal: *The Duality of Human Existence* (Chicago: Rand McNally, 1966), pp. 110–132. See also Sidney M. Jourard, "Some Lethal Aspects of the Male Role," in *The Transparent Self* (Princeton: D. Van Nostrand, 1964), Ch. 6.

7. This is described (with regrets) by Daniel Bell, "The Eclipse of Distance," *Encounter*, 20 (May 1963), 54–56; and Francis Fergusson, *The Idea of a Theater* (Princeton: Princeton University Press, 1949), especially pp. 92–93.

8. Here lies what I take to be the central distinction from what has become known as symbolic interactionism. The interactionist persuasion shared by such sociologists as Georg Simmel, George C. Homans, Herbert Blumer, Erving Goffman, and Howard S. Becker does not entail the kind of continuous self-reflective involvement of the social scientist which subverts all conclusions and cracks all theories. The armor of interactionism, unlike Don Quixote's, is not rusty; its prose, unlike Mailer's, is not breathless. (For a comprehensive discussion of the methods of interactionism, see Norman K. Denzin, *The Research Act* [Chicago: Aldine, 1970].)

Index

Acting. *See* Drama
Action, 102–104, 123–126, 128–130.
  See also Knowing as acting
Arendt, Hannah: on official language,
  47; on political foundations, 61–62;
  on political space, 62

Bacon, Francis, 25, 36, 43–44
Barthes, Roland, on irony, 100–101
Behavioralism. *See* Positivism
Benjamin, Walter, on translating, 101
Bentley, Arthur, 63–64
Berlin, Isaiah, on Vico, 67–69
Bertuccelli, Jean-Louis, review of
  film of, 114–118
Booth, Wayne, on authors and
  readers, 119

Change at Shebika (Duvignaud),
  critique of, 114–118
Children of Crisis (Coles), critique of,
  110–111
Coles, Robert, approach of, 110–111
Contextualism, 72–73, 125. *See also*
  Pragmatism

Deutsch, Karl, on political growth, 81
Dewey, John, 63–65
Dialectics, 128–129
Drama, 7–8, 111–112, 124–125, 149
Duvignaud, Jean, review of work of,
  114–118

Epistemology. *See* Knowing as acting

Equality, 118–119
Erikson, Erik, work of, 112–114
Ethnomethodology, 122
Etzioni, Amitai, epistemology of,
  85
Existentialism, 66
Experimentation, 57, 86–88, 120–126,
  128. *See also* Action; Pragmatism

Feldstein, Leonard C., on self-
  realization, 132–133

Garfinkel, Harold, on action, 122
Geertz, Clifford, on transactional
  praxis, 114–118
Gouldner, Alvin W.: on ethnomethodology, 122; on tragic drama,
  111–112

Harvey, O. J., on requisites for
  growth, 132
Herder, Johann Gottfried von,
  epistemology of, 69–70
Hobbes, Thomas, on individual
  action, 37, 94–95
Human nature, 83–84. *See also*
  Human needs; Political man
Human needs, 21–22, 62–63, 78, 82,
  84, 86–87, 90, 119. *See also*
  Political man

Ideology in political science. *See*
  Political science, dominant
  persuasion of

153

Institutions, political, 79–80, 97, 130–133
Interactionism, distinguished from transactionalism, 151
Irony, limits of, 99–102

James, William: on criterion for action, 80; on epistemology, 65–66; on minimal action, 127

Kant, Immanuel, 17, 19–21, 56–57
Knowing as acting, 65–75, 85–90, 93–99, 102–104, 113, 120–121. See also Language
Kuhn, Thomas S., on paradigm changes, 22–24

Language, 6, 17–22, 38, 40, 47, 65, 68, 71, 84–85, 96, 108–109, 121, 135–137

Machiavelli, Niccolò, and political creativity, 56
Marx, Karl: on ideology, 61; on necessity, 79–80
Mead, George Herbert, 64
Means and ends, 8, 35–36, 89
Mills, C. Wright, on releasing thought, 106–107

Natanson, Maurice, on philosophy as action, 104
Needs. See Human needs
Nietzsche, Friedrich: on creating reality, 118; on political creativity, 59–61

Paradigm, 2, 7; changes in, 22–24; in political science, 16. See also Political science
Plato, on contemplation, 93–94
Playing. See Drama
Pocock, J. G. A., on speech acts, 108–109
Political creativity, 55–62
Political institutions, 79–80, 97, 130–133

Political man, 78–79, 81–85, 90, 94. See also Human needs
Political science: conflicts in, 14–15, 40–41, 50–51, 144–145; dominant persuasion of, 2, 5, 26–27, 29–30, 38–40, 41–47, 51–53, 83, 90–91, 129 (see also Positivism); education in, 133–134; ideal mandates for, 5–6, 10–11, 54–55, 83, 85, 90, 98–99, 104, 106–112, 120–134, 135–136, 137–138 (see also Transactionalism)
Political space, 62–63, 72, 75, 80, 89–90
Positivism: background of, 32–34; examples of, 110–111; functions of, 41–47, 88–89, 96
Pragmatism, 63–64, 85–90
Psychoanalysis, 121–122

Ramparts of Clay (Bertuccelli), review of, 114–118
Reification, 7, 97–98, 129
Role-playing. See Drama

Schopenhauer, Arthur, on negative action, 58–59
Science, methods in, 22–25, 35–37, 64
Self and others, 5, 10. See also Drama
Skepticism, 55–56
Sorel, Georges, on need for myths, 61
Structure of Scientific Revolutions (Kuhn), 22–24
Symbolizing, 64–65, 70, 78. See also Language

Transactionalism, 10, 95–101, 103–104, 112–126, 135–136, 151. See also Knowing as acting

Vico, Giambattista, epistemology of, 67–69

Weber, Max, on contextualism, 72
Whorf, Benjamin Lee, on language, 20–21
Wolin, Sheldon S., on nonpolitical theories, 90

154